INTRODUCING
ISSUES WITH
OPPOSING
VIEWPOINTS®

Obesity

Lauri S. Friedman, *Book Editor*

D1518525

GREENHAVEN PRESS
A part of Gale, Cengage Learning

GALE
CENGAGE Learning·

Detroit • New York • San Francisco • New Haven, Conn • Waterville, Maine • London

GALE
CENGAGE Learning

Christine Nasso, *Publisher*
Elizabeth Des Chenes, *Managing Editor*

© 2011 Greenhaven Press, a part of Gale, Cengage Learning

Gale and Greenhaven Press are registered trademarks used herein under license.

For more information, contact:
Greenhaven Press
27500 Drake Rd.
Farmington Hills, MI 48331-3535
Or you can visit our Internet site at gale.cengage.com

ALL RIGHTS RESERVED.
No part of this work covered by the copyright herein may be reproduced, transmitted, stored, or used in any form or by any means graphic, electronic, or mechanical, including but not limited to photocopying, recording, scanning, digitizing, taping, Web distribution, information networks, or information storage and retrieval systems, except as permitted under Section 107 or 108 of the 1976 United States Copyright Act, without the prior written permission of the publisher.

For product information and technology assistance, contact us at

Gale Customer Support, 1-800-877-4253
For permission to use material from this text or product, submit all requests online at www.cengage.com/permissions

Further permissions questions can be e-mailed to permissionrequest@cengage.com

Articles in Greenhaven Press anthologies are often edited for length to meet page requirements. In addition, original titles of these works are changed to clearly present the main thesis and to explicitly indicate the author's opinion. Every effort is made to ensure that Greenhaven Press accurately reflects the original intent of the authors. Every effort has been made to trace the owners of copyrighted material.

Cover image © John Rensten/Corbis.

LIBRARY OF CONGRESS CATALOGING-IN-PUBLICATION DATA

Obesity / Lauri S. Friedman, book editor.
    p. cm. -- (Introducing issues with opposing viewpoints)
  Includes bibliographical references and index.
  ISBN 978-0-7377-5083-6 (hardcover)
  1. Obesity in children--United States--Popular works. 2. Obesity--Prevention--United States--Popular works. 3. Health promotion--United States--Popular works.
I. Friedman, Lauri S.
  RJ399.C6O324 2010
  618.92'398--dc22
                      2010028586

Printed in the United States of America
1 2 3 4 5 6 7 14 13 12 11 10

Contents

Foreword

I ndulging in a wide spectrum of ideas, beliefs, and perspectives is a critical cornerstone of democracy. After all, it is often debates over differences of opinion, such as whether to legalize abortion, how to treat prisoners, or when to enact the death penalty, that shape our society and drive it forward. Such diversity of thought is frequently regarded as the hallmark of a healthy and civilized culture. As the Reverend Clifford Schutjer of the First Congregational Church in Mansfield, Ohio, declared in a 2001 sermon, "Surrounding oneself with only like-minded people, restricting what we listen to or read only to what we find agreeable is irresponsible. Refusing to entertain doubts once we make up our minds is a subtle but deadly form of arrogance." With this advice in mind, Introducing Issues with Opposing Viewpoints books aim to open readers' minds to the critically divergent views that comprise our world's most important debates.

Introducing Issues with Opposing Viewpoints simplifies for students the enormous and often overwhelming mass of material now available via print and electronic media. Collected in every volume is an array of opinions that captures the essence of a particular controversy or topic. Introducing Issues with Opposing Viewpoints books embody the spirit of nineteenth-century journalist Charles A. Dana's axiom: "Fight for your opinions, but do not believe that they contain the whole truth, or the only truth." Absorbing such contrasting opinions teaches students to analyze the strength of an argument and compare it to its opposition. From this process readers can inform and strengthen their own opinions, or be exposed to new information that will change their minds. Introducing Issues with Opposing Viewpoints is a mosaic of different voices. The authors are statesmen, pundits, academics, journalists, corporations, and ordinary people who have felt compelled to share their experiences and ideas in a public forum. Their words have been collected from newspapers, journals, books, speeches, interviews, and the Internet, the fastest growing body of opinionated material in the world.

Introducing Issues with Opposing Viewpoints shares many of the well-known features of its critically acclaimed parent series, Opposing Viewpoints. The articles are presented in a pro/con format, allowing readers to absorb divergent perspectives side by side. Active reading questions preface each viewpoint, requiring the student to approach the material thoughtfully and carefully. Useful charts, graphs, and cartoons supplement each article. A thorough introduction provides readers with crucial background on an issue. An annotated bibliography points the reader toward articles, books, and Web sites that contain additional information on the topic. An appendix of organizations to contact contains a wide variety of charities, nonprofit organizations, political groups, and private enterprises that each hold a position on the issue at hand. Finally, a comprehensive index allows readers to locate content quickly and efficiently.

Introducing Issues with Opposing Viewpoints is also significantly different from Opposing Viewpoints. As the series title implies, its presentation will help introduce students to the concept of opposing viewpoints, and learn to use this material to aid in critical writing and debate. The series' four-color, accessible format makes the books attractive and inviting to readers of all levels. In addition, each viewpoint has been carefully edited to maximize a reader's understanding of the content. Short but thorough viewpoints capture the essence of an argument. A substantial, thought-provoking essay question placed at the end of each viewpoint asks the student to further investigate the issues raised in the viewpoint, compare and contrast two authors' arguments, or consider how one might go about forming an opinion on the topic at hand. Each viewpoint contains sidebars that include at-a-glance information and handy statistics. A Facts About section located in the back of the book further supplies students with relevant facts and figures.

Following in the tradition of the Opposing Viewpoints series, Greenhaven Press continues to provide readers with invaluable exposure to the controversial issues that shape our world. As John Stuart Mill once wrote: "The only way in which a human being can make some approach to knowing the whole of a subject is by hearing what can be said about it by persons of every variety of opinion and studying all modes in which it can be looked at by every character of mind. No wise man ever acquired his wisdom in any mode but this." It is to this principle that Introducing Issues with Opposing Viewpoints books are dedicated.

Introduction

When people talk about whether and to what extent the government should be involved in solving problems such as obesity, the term "nanny state" is invariably used. "Nanny state" is a derogatory term used by people who oppose government intervention in peoples' personal lives and daily habits. Campaigns to get people to drink or smoke less, taxes on fast food and soda, and laws against controversial but constitutionally protected behavior such as gun ownership are all good examples of efforts dubbed "nanny state initiatives" by opponents. Whether the government has a positive role to play in reducing obesity or whether state-sponsored obesity initiatives constitute improper intrusion into Americans' personal lives is hotly debated by politicians, academics, health specialists, lobbyists, and others.

Opponents of government initiatives to reduce obesity argue that being overweight is a personal problem and thus the responsibility of the overweight person to solve. A 2009 campaign by First Lady Michelle Obama to reduce childhood obesity, for example, was chided by nanny state opponents as being ineffective and inappropriate. "Good intentions aside, a presidential task force isn't going to do what millions of American parents already don't do," writes Marybeth Hicks. "Namely, pull the plug on the 68 percent of kids with televisions in their bedrooms, or on the average 53 hours per week [they] spend engaged with electronic media. Nor will the task force change the way most families eat."[1] Hicks resents the fact that more than seven governmental Web sites are devoted to nutrition advocacy, which she says indicates the government is overly involved in this private area of its citizens lives—and without much positive effect. "The subject of nutrition alone already enjoys millions of dollars in government Internet attention—never mind the countless publications, pamphlets and educational programs. Clearly, there is nothing about eating that the U.S. government isn't already telling us, so maybe that's not the problem."[2]

For Hicks and others, the government has no business telling Americans how to eat and live: That is the job—and right—of people themselves. Indeed, personal responsibility is at the heart of reasons why Hicks and others will never support obesity prevention initiatives such as taxing junk food or banning fast-food restaurants. Sara Wexler, of the conservative American Enterprise Institute, which opposes unnecessary government intervention, has put the matter in the following way: "Banning fast-food restaurants will not solve the obesity problem, nor will any other laws that scapegoat the food industry and ignore personal responsibility."[3]

Another argument against government regulation of obesity is that as a free people, Americans have the right to eat what they like, regardless of whether it is unhealthy or fattening. For this reason, nanny state opponents such as journalist Rob Lyons oppose government campaigns that would force restaurants to post nutritional information on their menus. "Food should be both sustenance *and* pleasure. The demand that we constantly check our desires against some government-imposed calorie-related target robs us of this joy, replacing it with guilt and fear instead," says Lyons. "Rather than labeling everything we eat with calorie and fat contents, a far healthier attitude would be to leave us to make up our own minds about what we consume."[4]

Yet many Americans welcome government intervention on a problem like obesity, arguing that just as it is the government's responsibility to protect us from terrorism and crime, so too should it be the government's job to protect us from products that are known to cause illness, such as cigarettes and unhealthy food. Supporters of government-sponsored obesity prevention programs argue it is irresponsible to accept public involvement and guidance on certain issues but not others. Dan Mitchell, a writer for the *New York Times* and the *Chicago Tribune*, puts the issue in the following way: "[A nanny state opponent] believes that it's OK for schools to teach algebra and—more to the point—health and physical education. But at the same time he believes teaching that eating garbage is bad for you should be left solely to parents."[5] Mitchell and others argue it is unfair to pick and choose which issues the government should be involved with and believe the government has an important and positive role to play in helping people make healthier choices about their food.

Furthermore, obesity is such a complex problem with so many causes, Americans like writer Marc Ambinder think its solution can only be "the province of policy makers: state legislatures, school boards, members of Congress, executive-branch members, even corporate boards."[6] This is because such entities are the only ones with the resources, budgets, and influence to effect change on this multi–faceted, far-reaching problem. Indeed, obesity is rarely simply a problem of eating too much and exercising too little. Some have pointed to the insidious nature of junk- and fast-food marketing as a cause; others blame the sprawling design of American communities that require driving rather than walking or biking. Combined with the fact that most American jobs promote a sedentary lifestyle and the fact that increased portion sizes have resulted in Americans taking in five hundred more calories per day than they did forty years ago, obesity appears to be not merely a personal problem but a systemic one. Because obesity has so many external causes, people like Ambinder think it is too much to expect people to be able to combat it on their own: "Putting individual solutions and free will up against the increase in portion sizes, massive technological and societal changes, food-company taste-engineering, and the ubiquity of effective television advertisements is like asking Ecuador to conquer China."[7] Simply put, obesity prevention requires an enormous effort that the government is uniquely capable of tackling.

Finally, as obesity plagues increasing numbers of Americans, supporters argue that the government has the right to intervene because it is directly affected by the problem. The burden that overweight and obese people place on the health care system grows each year and is accompanied by a daunting price tag. A 2009 study by the Centers for Disease Control and Prevention, for example, found that obesity-related health expenses cost the United States as much as $147 billion each year. By 2020, according to the Rand Corporation, a nonprofit public policy organization, obesity-related problems will account for more than one-fifth of national health care costs. Thus, from a financial perspective, the government has a vested interest in keeping its citizens trim and healthy. Rather than nannying or nagging its citizens, supporters argue the government is merely doing the main job with which it is charged: keeping its citizens safe while responsibly spending their tax dollars.

Whether and to what extent the government should be involved in finding solutions to obesity is just one of the many topics debated in *Introducing Issues with Opposing Viewpoints: Obesity*. Pro/con article pairs also explore whether restaurants should be required to post nutritional information, what measures schools should take to curb childhood obesity, whether junk food should be taxed, and whether overweight people should have to pay more for health insurance. The guided reading questions and essay prompts encourage readers to develop their own opinions on this issue of ongoing importance.

Notes

1. Marybeth Hicks, "Child Obesity in Nanny State," *Washington Times*, February 24, 2010. www.washingtontimes.com/news/2010/feb/24/hicks-child-obesity-in-nanny-state/
2. Hicks, "Child Obesity in Nanny State."
3. Sara Wexler, "Fat Chance," *American*, August 21, 2008. www.american.com/archive/2008/august-08-08/fat-chance.
4. Rob Lyons, "Calorie-Counting Is an Eating Disorder," *Spiked*, April 8, 2009. www.spiked-online.com/index.php/site/article/6441.
5. Dan Mitchell, "Democrats Want to Ban School Junk Food," The Big Money Daily Bread Blog, *Slate*, February 8, 2010. www.thebigmoney.com/blogs/daily-bread/2010/02/08/democrats-introduce-junk-food-ban-schools?page=full.
6. Marc Ambinder, "Beating Obesity," *Atlantic*, May 2010. www.theatlantic.com/magazine/archive/2010/04/beating-obesity/8017.
7. Ambinder, "Beating Obesity," pp. 77–78.

Chapter 1

Is Obesity a Serious Problem?

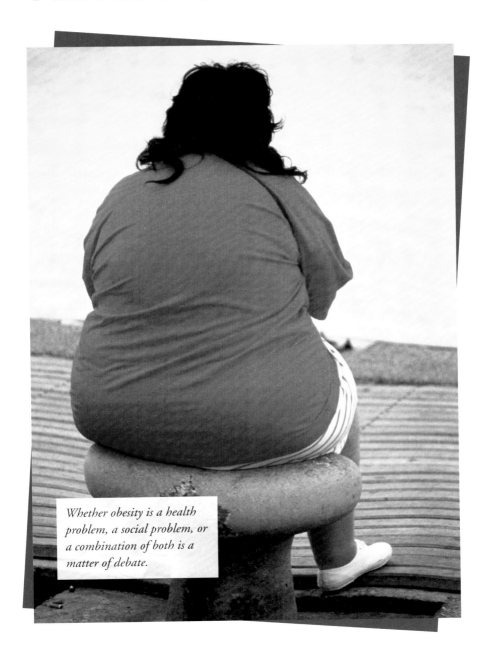

Whether obesity is a health problem, a social problem, or a combination of both is a matter of debate.

Viewpoint

1

Obesity Is a Serious Problem

Trust for America's Health

"During the past 30 years, adult obesity rates have doubled and childhood obesity rates have more than tripled."

Trust for America's Health is an advocacy organization that seeks to prevent disease and protect the health and safety of communities. In the following viewpoint it argues that obesity is a serious problem for Americans. American obesity rates have risen in the last thirty years, costing Americans health, happiness, money, and productivity. The author explains that the American lifestyle has contributed significantly to the rise in obesity—Americans walk less, eat more, consume more junk food, and spend more time in front of televisions and computers than ever before. Because Americans are overweight, they develop diseases at a higher rate, which, in addition to being expensive to treat and unpleasant to experience, causes them to be less productive as workers. For all of these reasons, the author urges Americans to make lifestyle changes that will help them lose weight and encourages the government to support programs that will help people in this endeavor.

F as in Fat: How Obesity Policies Are Failing in America. Princeton, NJ: Trust for America's Health and Robert Wood Johnson Foundation, 2009. Reproduced by permission of the publishers.

AS YOU READ, CONSIDER THE FOLLOWING QUESTIONS:
  1. How much lower does the author say health care spending would be per person had obesity rates not risen as much as they have?
  2. In how many states does the author say obesity rates rose in 2008–2009? In how many states did they decline?
  3. Name at least four American trends the author says have contributed to rising obesity rates.

The obesity epidemic is harming the health of millions of Americans and resulting in billions of additional dollars in health care costs. Rising rates of obesity over the past few decades are one of the major factors behind the skyrocketing rates of health care costs in the United States. And, U.S. economic competitiveness is hurting as our workforce has become less healthy and less productive. During the past 30 years, adult obesity rates have doubled and childhood obesity rates have more than tripled, while health spending has increased two percentage points faster than the Gross Domestic Product (GDP), growing from 8.8 percent in 1980 to a projected 17.6 percent in 2009.

Experts estimate that more than a quarter of America's health care costs are related to obesity. The sharp rise in obesity has accounted for 20 to 30 percent of the rise in health care spending since 1979. Had obesity rates remained stable, health care spending in America would be nearly 10 percent lower on a per person average. The country will never be able to contain rates of chronic diseases and health care costs until we find ways to keep Americans healthier. But right now, Americans are not as healthy as they could be or should be. Two-thirds of adults are overweight or obese. The childhood obesity epidemic is putting today's youth on course to potentially be the first generation to live shorter, less healthy lives than their parents. . . .

In the past year [2008–2009], adult obesity rates grew in 23 states and did not decrease in a single state. The number of obese adults now exceeds 25 percent in nearly two-thirds of states. In 1991, no state had an obesity rate above 20 percent. In 1980, the national average of obese adults was 15 percent.

And, obesity rates are likely to grow even more in the next year due to the economic downturn, which has a negative impact on the health of Americans. Americans increasingly need to balance concerns about their pocketbooks against managing their health. Food prices are projected to rise five percent in 2009, according to the U.S. Department of Agriculture (USDA), and nutritious foods are becoming increasingly out of reach for even middle-income families. Depression and anxiety are linked with obesity for many, while stress and the strain of limited resources can make it harder for many to find the time to be physically active. At the same time, safety-net programs and services are becoming increasingly overextended as the numbers of unemployed, uninsured and underinsured continue to grow.

FAST FACT

According to the World Health Organization, as of 2010 more than 1 billion adults were overweight, at least 300 million of them obese.

As a nation, if we made combating obesity a national priority, we could have a tremendous pay-off in improving health and reducing health care costs. A greater emphasis is needed on developing strategies, policies, and programs to help make it easier for more Americans to improve the quality of what we eat, limit the quantity of what we eat and engage in more physical activity.

While individuals have choices about what they eat or how active they are, these decisions are affected by factors that are beyond individual control, which is why policies and resources in communities are so important. For instance, in neighborhoods with limited grocery stores or unsafe parks, it is hard for people to eat healthy foods and be physically active. Many of these factors are directly related to economic circumstances.

The rising obesity rates are the result of a number of trends in the United States:

- Americans consume an average of 300 more calories per day than they did 25 years ago and eat less nutritious foods;
- Nutritious foods are significantly more expensive than calorie-dense, less nutritious foods;

- Americans walk less and drive more—even for trips of less than one mile;
- Parks and recreation spaces are not considered safe or well maintained in many communities;
- Many school lunches do not meet nutrition standards and children engage in less physical activity in school;
- Increased screen time (TV, computers, video games) contributes to decreased activity, particularly for children; and
- Adults often work longer hours and commute farther.

The World's Fattest Countries

The United States ranks as the third fattest nation on the planet. More than two-thirds of its population is classified as overweight. Worldwide more than 1 billion adults are overweight, and at least 300 million of these are obese.

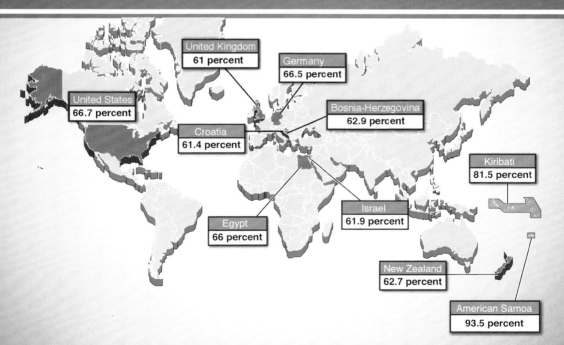

United Kingdom
61 percent

Germany
66.5 percent

United States
66.7 percent

Bosnia-Herzegovina
62.9 percent

Croatia
61.4 percent

Kiribati
81.5 percent

Israel
61.9 percent

Egypt
66 percent

New Zealand
62.7 percent

American Samoa
93.5 percent

Taken from: World Health Organization, 2008.

Americans eat less nutritious foods and consume three hundred more calories per day then they did twenty-five years ago.

The obesity crisis is a national problem. The health and economic consequences impact the entire country—and the future health and wealth of the nation requires that we treat the obesity problem with the urgency it deserves.

The federal government, states, and communities around the country have taken action to address the obesity epidemic, but—even before the precipitous economic downturn—these actions were constrained due to limited resources. These policies and programs address factors such as the availability or affordability of healthy food; the safety and accessibility of parks; the amount of time students get for physical activity; and the nutritional quality of school lunches. These efforts are aimed at helping make healthy choices easier for Americans.

While the obesity epidemic may seem hard to address on a big-picture level, research shows that small changes can result in major improvements in the health of individuals, and these improvements, in turn, can help to reduce health care costs. For example:

- For individuals, a five percent to 10 percent reduction in total weight can lead to positive health benefits, such as reducing the risk for type 2 diabetes, and
- An increase in physical activity, even without any accompanying weight loss, can contribute to significant health improvements. A physically active lifestyle plays an important role in preventing many chronic diseases, including heart disease, hypertension, and type 2 diabetes.

On a community level, a small investment in programs to improve nutrition and physical activity can result in a big payoff in a short time frame. A recent study by the Trust for America's Health (TFAH) found that an investment of just $10 per person per year in proven community-based disease prevention programs could save the country more than $16 billion annually within five years. This is a return of $5.60 for every $1.

This finding, which is based on an economic model developed by the Urban Institute and an extensive review of evidence-based studies by The New York Academy of Medicine, found that such an investment could reduce rates of type 2 diabetes and high blood pressure by five percent within just two years; rates of heart disease, stroke and kidney disease by five percent within five years; and rates of some types of cancer, arthritis and chronic obstructive pulmonary disease by 2.5 percent within 10 to 20 years.

EVALUATING THE AUTHOR'S ARGUMENTS:

In this viewpoint Trust for America's Health uses statistics, facts, and examples to make its argument that obesity is a serious problem for Americans. The organization does not, however, use any quotations to support its points. If you were to rewrite this article and insert quotations, what authorities might you quote from? Where would you place these quotations to bolster the points made by the organization?

Obesity Is Not a Serious Problem

Patrick Basham and John Luik

"The evidence is now flooding in from both America and England that obesity is the epidemic that never was."

In the following viewpoint Patrick Basham and John Luik argue that the problem of obesity has been largely exaggerated. They point to study data that show that contrary to popular opinion, America never experienced a public obesity crisis. They say that adult men and women and most segments of children did not experience statistically significant increases in obesity in the last decade, and some segments of the population even experienced lower levels of obesity. Basham and Luik say not only did the obesity epidemic never actually exist, but attacks on junk food and fast-food advertising have been baseless. They conclude the government has exaggerated the seriousness of obesity and based its treatment programs on false information.

Basham and Luik are coauthors of the book *Diet Nation: Exposing the Obesity Crusade.* Basham is the director of the Democracy Institute, where Luik is a senior fellow.

Patrick Basham and John Luik, "The Myth of an 'Obesity Tsunami,'" *spiked-online.com*, January 19, 2010. Copyright © *spiked* 2010. All rights reserved. Reproduced by permission.

AS YOU READ, CONSIDER THE FOLLOWING QUESTIONS:
1. What is the National Health and Nutrition Examination Survey and what did it measure?
2. Who experienced a decrease in obesity between 2005 and 2006, according to the authors?
3. What does the term "nanny state" mean in the context of the viewpoint?

E veryone knows The Truth about obesity: we're getting fatter each year. Our growing girth is termed everything from the "pandemic of the twenty-first century" to an "obesity tsunami." But the evidence is now flooding in from both America and England that obesity is the epidemic that never was.

The Epidemic That Never Was

Two studies produced by the US Centers for Disease Control and Prevention (CDC) and published last week [in January 2010] in the *Journal of the American Medical Association*—one about obesity in children and adolescents, and the other about adult obesity—completely undermine the claims of an obesity epidemic.

Both studies are based on information from the National Health and Nutrition Examination Survey from 2007–08, which is a representative sample of the American population. The survey measured the heights and weights of 3,281 children and adolescents and 219 infants and toddlers, as well as 5,555 adult women and men. The study of children and adolescents looked at the body mass index (BMI) of children and adolescents over five time periods between 1999 and 2008, the decade during which child obesity was widely described as America's preeminent public health problem.

> ## FAST FACT
>
> When researchers at the University at Buffalo School of Medicine and Biomedical Sciences examined records of more than sixty-two thousand patients in intensive-care units in the United States, Europe, Australia, and the Middle East, they found that just 25 percent were obese.

The results are striking. During none of the five periods was there a statistically significant trend, except for boys at the highest BMI levels. In other words, if there was a spike in obesity, it was confined to a very small number of very obese boys.

No Statistically Significant Changes

What about the adult "couch potato" generation? Here, again, the results put the lie to claims of an obesity tsunami. In the study of adults, the researchers also looked at obesity trends over the past decade. For women, there were no statistically significant changes in obesity prevalence over the entire decade, while for men there were no prevalent differences during the last five years of the decade. As the researchers note, obesity prevalence may have "entered another period of relative stability."

A similar absence of an obesity epidemic is to be found in England. According to the Health Survey for England, which collected data from 7,500 children and almost 7,000 adults, there has been a decline in the prevalence of overweight and obesity for adult men, while for adult women prevalence has remained the same.

Comparing the results of the survey for 2007 with those of 2004, there have been either declines or no significant changes in male prevalence of

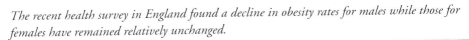

The recent health survey in England found a decline in obesity rates for males while those for females have remained relatively unchanged.

When asked what they thought was the biggest health problem facing the country, most Americans did not say obesity.

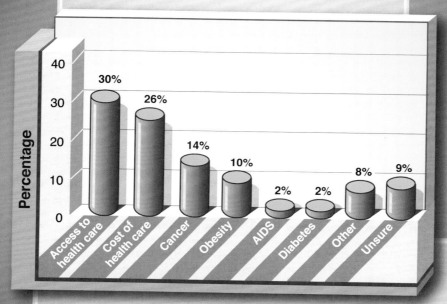

Question: "What would you say is the most urgent health problem facing this country at the present time?"

Taken from: Gallup poll, November 11–14, 2007.

overweight and obesity in all age groups from 16–54. As for children, the survey finds: "There was no significant change in mean BMI over-weight/obesity prevalence between 2006 and 2007, and there are indications that the trend in obesity prevalence may have begun to flatten out over the last two to three years."

Overweight and Obesity Have Declined in Some Groups

For example, there was a decrease in obesity in girls aged two to 15 years old between 2005 and 2006, from 18 per cent in 2005 to 15 per cent in 2006. Among boys aged two to 10 years old, the prevalence of overweight declined from 16 per cent in 2005 to 12 per cent in 2006. According to the results, overweight and obesity have been declining amongst boys and girls aged two to 15 since 2004. In girls, obesity prevalence levels are largely unchanged from where they were in 2001.

Junk Food and Soda Do Not Cause Obesity

The findings of the English survey not only contradict the claim that we are in the midst of an obesity epidemic, but they also debunk the public health establishment's erroneous claim that increases in children's weight are due to junkfood advertising and too many sugary soda drinks. According to the survey, the root cause of any weight gains that one does see appear to lie in physical activity levels. For example, "21 per cent of girls aged two to 15 in the low physical-activity group were classed as obese compared with 15 per cent of the high group."

A similar pattern was found in the 2006 survey, which found that 33 per cent of girls aged two to 15 with low levels of physical activity were either overweight or obese compared with 27 per cent of those with high levels of physical activity. As with smoking, obesity prevalence was higher in both boys and girls in the lowest income group.

Clearly, governments' current course of draconian [exceedingly harsh] regulatory treatment seeks to cure an illusory disease. The nanny state's infatuation with an obesity epidemic that does not exist is a searing indictment of this particular public health crusade.

> ## EVALUATING THE AUTHORS' ARGUMENTS:
>
> Both Basham and Luik and Trust for America's Health, author of the previous viewpoint, used statistics to support their argument. Yet each set of authors used different sets of statistics and came to different conclusions about the seriousness of the obesity problem. Examine each viewpoint and identify the source of these statistics. In your opinion, which set of statistics is more convincing? Why?

Obesity Carries Serious Health Risks

Weight Control Information Network

"Being over-weight may increase the risk of developing several types of cancer, including cancers of the colon, esophagus, and kidney."

The following viewpoint was written by Weight Control Information Network, the branch of the government charged with safeguarding the U.S. public's health. The department argues that obesity causes serious health risks. It discusses how overweight and obese people are more at risk for cancer, heart disease, diabetes, gallbladder disease, sleep apnea, osteoarthritis, and other serious disorders. Losing just 10 or 20 pounds can significantly reduce a person's chances for developing obesity-related diseases, according to the author.

Weight Control Information Network. "Do You Know the Health Risks of Being Overweight?" Weight Control Information Network: An Information Service of the National Institute of Diabetes and Digestive and Kidney Diseases (NIDDK), December, 2007. Reproduced by permission.

1. How can weight loss reduce a person's chance for developing heart disease?
2. What is metabolic syndrome, and how has it been linked to obesity?
3. Why is an overweight person more at risk for sleep apnea?

Weighing too much may increase your risk for developing many health problems. If you are overweight or obese, you may be at risk for:

- type 2 diabetes
- coronary heart disease and stroke
- metabolic syndrome
- certain types of cancer
- sleep apnea
- osteoarthritis
- gallbladder disease
- fatty liver disease
- pregnancy complications . . .

Type 2 Diabetes

Type 2 diabetes is a disease in which blood sugar levels are above normal. High blood sugar is a major cause of coronary heart disease, kidney disease, stroke, amputation, and blindness. In 2002, diabetes was the sixth leading cause of death in the United States.

Type 2 diabetes is the most common type of diabetes in the United States. This form of diabetes is most often associated with old age, obesity, family history of diabetes, previous history of gestational diabetes, and physical inactivity. The disease is more common among certain ethnic populations.

More than 85 percent of people with type 2 diabetes are overweight. It is not known exactly why people who are overweight are more likely to develop this disease. It may be that being overweight causes cells to change, making them resistant to the hormone insulin. Insulin carries sugar from blood to the cells, where it is used for energy. When a person is insulin resistant, blood sugar cannot be taken up by the

A prick of blood is taken for a type 2 diabetes test. Eighty-five percent of the people with type 2 diabetes are obese or overweight.

cells, resulting in high blood sugar. In addition, the cells that produce insulin must work extra hard to try to keep blood sugar normal. This may cause these cells to gradually fail. . . .

Coronary Heart Disease and Stroke

Coronary heart disease means that the heart and circulation (blood flow) are not functioning normally. Often, the arteries have become hardened and narrowed. If you have coronary heart disease, you may suffer from a heart attack, congestive heart failure, sudden cardiac death, angina (chest pain), or abnormal heart rhythm. In a heart attack, the flow of blood and oxygen to the heart is disrupted, damaging portions of the heart muscle. During a stroke, blood and oxygen do not flow normally to the brain, possibly causing paralysis or death. Coronary heart disease is the leading cause of death in the United States, and stroke is the third leading cause.

People who are overweight are more likely to develop high blood pressure, high levels of triglycerides (blood fats) and LDL cholesterol (a fat-like substance often called "bad cholesterol"), and low levels of HDL cholesterol ("good cholesterol"). These are all risk factors for heart disease and stroke. In addition, excess body fat—especially abdominal fat—may produce substances that cause inflammation. Inflammation in blood vessels and throughout the body may raise heart disease risk.

Losing 5 to 10 percent of your weight can lower your chances for developing coronary heart disease or having a stroke. If you weigh 200 pounds, this means losing as little as 10 pounds. Weight loss may improve blood pressure, triglyceride, and cholesterol levels; improve heart function and blood flow; and decrease inflammation throughout the body.

Metabolic Syndrome

The metabolic syndrome is a group of obesity-related risk factors for coronary heart disease and diabetes. A person has the metabolic syndrome if he or she has three or more of the following risk factors:

- A large waistline. For men, this means a waist measurement of 40 inches or more. For women, it means a waist measurement of 35 inches or more.
- High triglycerides or taking medication to treat high triglycerides. A triglyceride level of 150 mg/dL or higher is considered high.
- Low levels of HDL ("good") cholesterol or taking medications to treat low HDL. For men, low HDL cholesterol is below 40 mg/dL. For women, it is below 50 mg/dL.
- High blood pressure or taking medications to treat high blood pressure. High blood pressure is 130 mm Hg or higher for systolic blood pressure (the top number) or 85 mm Hg or higher for diastolic blood pressure (the bottom number)
- High fasting blood glucose (sugar) or taking medications to treat high blood sugar. This means a fasting blood sugar of 100 mg/dL or higher.

A person with metabolic syndrome has approximately twice the risk for coronary heart disease and five times the risk for type 2 diabetes. It is estimated that 27 percent of American adults have the metabolic syndrome.

The metabolic syndrome is strongly linked to obesity, especially abdominal obesity. Other risk factors are physical inactivity, insulin resistance, genetics, and old age.

Obesity is a risk factor for the metabolic syndrome because it raises blood pressure and triglycerides, lowers good cholesterol, and contributes to insulin resistance. Excess fat around the abdomen carries even higher risks. . . .

Cancer

Cancer occurs when cells in one part of the body, such as the colon, grow abnormally or out of control. The cancerous cells sometimes spread to other parts of the body, such as the liver. Cancer is the second leading cause of death in the United States.

Being overweight may increase the risk of developing several types of cancer, including cancers of the colon, esophagus, and kidney. Overweight is also linked with uterine and postmenopausal breast cancer in women. Gaining weight during adult life increases the risk for several of these cancers, even if the weight gain does not result in overweight or obesity.

It is not known exactly how being overweight increases cancer risk. It may be that fat cells release hormones that affect cell growth, leading to cancer. Also, eating or physical activity habits that may lead to being overweight may also contribute to cancer risk. . . .

FAST FACT

A study published in the February 2010 issue of the *American Journal of Preventive Medicine* found that the Quality-Adjusted Life Years (QALYs)—a measurement of both the quality and quantity of human life—lost due to obesity is now equal to, if not greater than, those lost due to smoking.

Sleep Apnea

Sleep apnea is a condition in which a person stops breathing for short periods during the night. A person who has sleep apnea may suffer from daytime sleepiness, difficulty concentrating, and even heart failure.

The risk for sleep apnea is higher for people who are overweight. A person who is overweight may have more fat stored around his or her neck. This may make the airway smaller. A smaller airway can make breathing difficult, loud (snoring), or stop altogether. In addition, fat stored in the neck and throughout the body may produce

Obesity Is Linked to a Significant Increase in Chronic Conditions

Obesity is linked to very high rates of chronic illnesses—higher than living in poverty, and much higher than smoking or drinking. When compared with normal-weight individuals of the same age and sex having similar social demographics, obese people suffer from an increase in chronic conditions of approximately 67 percent. In contrast, the increase for normal-weight daily smokers is only 25 percent and for normal-weight heavy drinkers, only 12 percent.

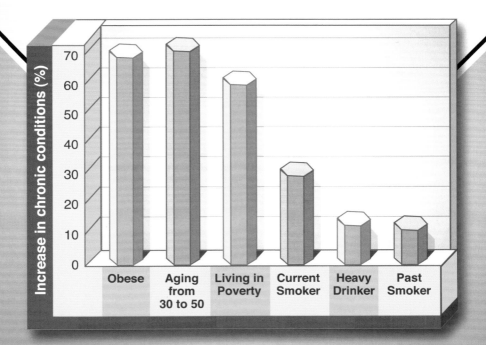

Baseline = comparable normal-weight individuals with no history of smoking or heavy drinking.

Taken from: "The Health Risks of Obesity: Worse than Smoking, Drinking, or Poverty," RAND Health, 2002, p.2.

substances that cause inflammation. Inflammation in the neck is a risk factor for sleep apnea.

Osteoarthritis

Osteoarthritis is a common joint disorder that causes the joint bone and cartilage (tissue that protects joints) to wear away. Osteoarthritis most often affects the joints of the knees, hips, and lower back.

Extra weight may place extra pressure on joints and cartilage, causing them to wear away. In addition, people with more body fat may have higher blood levels of substances that cause inflammation. Inflammation at the joints may raise the risk for osteoarthritis.

Weight loss of at least 5 percent of your body weight may decrease stress on your knees, hips, and lower back, and lessen inflammation in your body. If you have osteoarthritis, losing weight may help improve your symptoms.

Gallbladder Disease

Gallbladder disease includes gallstones and inflammation or infection of the gallbladder. Gallstones are clusters of solid material that form in the gallbladder. They are made mostly of cholesterol and can cause abdominal pain, especially after consuming fatty foods. The pain may be sharp or dull.

People who are overweight have a higher risk for developing gallbladder disease. They may produce more cholesterol (a fat-like substance found in the body), a risk factor for gallstones. Also, people who are overweight may have an enlarged gallbladder, which may not work properly.

EVALUATING THE AUTHORS' ARGUMENTS:

This viewpoint was published by a branch of the U.S. government. Does the fact that it is a government document influence your opinion of its credibility? Why or why not? Write one or two paragraphs on whether you think the government is a trusted source for obesity information. Then write one or two sentences for each author in this chapter on what each would think about whether the government is a trusted source for information on obesity.

Viewpoint

4

The Health Risks of Obesity Have Been Overstated

Jacob Sullum

"Except for certain conditions associated with very high BMIs . . . , there is little evidence that extra weight per se causes health problems."

In the following viewpoint, Jacob Sullum reviews two books that evaluate the claims of extreme health risks associated with obesity, claims that were supported by the Centers for Disease Control and Prevention in 2004. The authors reviewed find that the correlation between obesity and illness depends primarily on poor diet and lack of exercise, which are factors that independently increase the risk of heart disease and diabetes. In addition, the authors reviewed find that the point on the body mass index rating scale at which a person is considered obese is not based on medical evidence of increased mortality rate and that the methods that obesity researchers use tend to skew their results in favor of showing increased health risks from obesity.

Jacob Sullum, "Lay Off the Fatties: They're Not Hurting Anybody—Maybe Not Even Themselves *(Fat Politics: The Real Story Behind America's Obesity Epidemic) (The Diet Myth: Why America's Obsession with Weight Is Hazardous to Your Health)* (Book Review)," *Reason*, November 2006, pp. 74ff. Copyright © 2006 Reason Foundation. Reproduced with permission.

Jacob Sullum is a senior editor at *Reason* magazine. He is the author of *For Your Own Good: The Anti-smoking Crusade and the Tyranny of Public Health.*

AS YOU READ, CONSIDER THE FOLLOWING QUESTIONS:
1. According to the author, in 2004 how many people did the Centers for Disease Control and Prevention report had died from poor diet and physical inactivity; what was the figure one year later?
2. What number on the BMI rating scale marks the lower level of the obesity range, according to Sullum?
3. According to the author, what strategies does author Paul Campos say are used by people who profit from the War on Fat?

The government seems to have made tremendous strides in its War on Fat. In 2004 researchers at the U.S. Centers for Disease Control and Prevention (CDC) said "poor diet and physical inactivity" were killing 400,000 Americans a year, a number that was widely presented as an estimate of "obesity-related deaths." Just one year later, the estimate had been reduced to about 100,000. To cut the death toll by 75 percent in the space of a year, the anti-fat crusaders must be doing something right.

Or something wrong. Ascribing deaths from chronic diseases to specific lifestyle variables is a tricky, highly uncertain business, and the 400,000 figure, which was announced in *The Journal of the American Medical Association* by a team that included the director of the CDC, was suspect from the start. For one thing, the association between fatness and mortality disappears among Americans 65 and older, the age group that accounts for most deaths. According to the CDC's own data for the years 2001 to 2003, excluding older Americans leaves just 585,000 or so deaths a year, of which more than 180,000 are caused by accidents, suicide, homicide, lung cancer, HIV, influenza, pneumonia, and chronic lower respiratory diseases—none of which the CDC blames on obesity. To believe the 400,000 death toll, you'd have to believe that virtually all the remaining deaths, from causes such as heart disease, stroke, hypertension, cancer, and diabetes, are due to "poor diet and physical inactivity," a phrase public health officials and the press have treated as synonymous with fatness. (More on that later.) That would leave no room for risk factors such as smoking, stress, and heredity.

It did not take long for another set of government-employed statisticians to issue a new, much lower estimate of mortality due to excessive weight, this one also published in *JAMA*. By their reckoning, obesity—meaning a body mass index (BMI) of 30 or more, corresponding to a weight of 203 pounds or more for a man of average height (five feet, nine inches)—accounts for 112,000 deaths a year in the U.S. But in this study, people who were merely "overweight," with BMIs between 25 and 30 (meaning a weight between 169 and 202 pounds for an average-height man), did not have higher mortality than people of "normal" or "ideal" weight, which is in fact neither normal (since most Americans exceed it) nor, to judge by this study, ideal in terms of health. In fact, the death rate among chubby (but not obese) people in this study was lower than the death rate among thin (but not underweight) people, to the tune of 86,000 fewer deaths a year. Which makes you wonder exactly what it means to be "overweight" and why we should be worried about it.

University of Chicago political scientist J. Eric Oliver, author of *Fat Politics*, and University of Colorado law professor Paul Campos, author of *The Diet Myth* (published in hard-cover as *The Obesity Myth*), both take up this question, and they reach similar conclusions. First and foremost, they argue that, except for certain conditions associated with very high BMIs (starting around 4%, which corresponds to a weight of 271 pounds for an average-height man), there is little evidence that extra weight per se causes health problems. To the extent that fatness is correlated with illness, they maintain, it is primarily because fatness is associated with "poor diet and inactivity"— factors that independently raise the risk of diabetes, high blood pressure, cancer, and cardiovascular disease. Fat people are less likely than thin people to exercise regularly, and they are more likely to skimp on fruits, vegetables, and whole grains while eating diets high in fat and refined carbohydrates. Oliver and Campos say these habits, which are more common among fat people but shared by many thin people, are the main problem. Campos also emphasizes the health risks of repeatedly losing and regaining weight. Overall, Oliver and Campos, both of whom say they accepted the conventional wisdom about weight at the outset of their research, make a persuasive case for their contrarian stance.

Having shown that the medical case against fatness is much weaker than government officials and anti-obesity activists claim, Oliver and Campos ask why it is pushed so aggressively and accepted so widely. They see motivations ranging from the rational (the vested interests of obesity researchers, public health officials, and the diet and pharmaceutical industries) to the irrational (a deep-seated cultural revulsion at fat people, disproportionately poor symbols of sloth who serve as stand-ins for minority scapegoats). Here, too, Oliver and Campos are pretty persuasive, but from a policy perspective their analyses are ultimately unsatisfying. Assuming they are right that fatness per se is the wrong target, that the real threats to our health are poor nutrition and sedentary lifestyles, the question remains: What is the government's proper role in addressing these threats?

While neither Oliver nor Campos seems inclined to favor interventions aimed at getting us to eat better and exercise more, neither do they take a clear, principled stand against them. In particular, they do not directly challenge the slippery "public health" reasoning that treats risky behavior like a contagious disease, providing an open-ended excuse for government meddling in formerly private decisions. The same rationale that makes smoking, drinking, drug use, driving without a seat belt, or biking without a helmet a "public health" issue—the government's purported duty to discourage actions that may lead to disease or injury—applies with equal force to diet, exercise, and every other lifestyle variable that affects morbidity and mortality.

Although neither Oliver nor Campos launches a broad attack on this agenda, they do an effective job of questioning the reality of the "obesity epidemic," beginning with the very definition of overweight and obese. "Fat," says Campos, "is a cultural construct, not a medical fact." In 1985, Oliver notes, a consensus conference convened by the National Institutes of Health (NIH) recommended that men and women be considered "overweight" at BMIs of 27.8 and 27.3, respectively. In 1996 an NIH-sponsored review of the literature found that "increased mortality typically was not evident until well beyond a BMI level of 30." Yet two years later, the NIH yielded to a World Health Organization recommendation that "overweight" be defined downward to a BMI of 25, with 30 or more qualifying as "obese." Oliver says "the scientific 'evidence' to justify this change"—which made millions of Americans overweight overnight—"was nonexistent" since "there is no uniform point on the BMI scale where all these diseases [linked to weight] become more evident."

Moving beyond correlation to causation, things get even more complicated. Campos and Oliver complain that obesity researchers are so eager to demonstrate a link between fatness and sickness that they routinely make the sort of statistical adjustments that strengthen the association but rarely make the sort that would weaken it. For example, studies generally control for smoking, an independent cause of disease that is more common among thin people, and pre-existing illnesses, which might make thin people look unhealthy because people tend to lose weight when they're sick. But obesity researchers usually do not take into account fitness levels, nutrition, yo-yo dieting, and the side effects of weight loss drugs.

"Nearly all the warnings about obesity are based on little more than loose statistical conjecture," says Oliver, adding that there is no plausible biological explanation for most of the asserted causal links between fatness and disease. "The health risks associated with increasing weight are generally small," says Campos, and "these risks tend to disappear altogether when factors other than weight are taken into account." For example, "a moderately active larger person is likely to be far healthier than someone who is svelte but sedentary." Campos cites research finding that obese people "who engage in at least moderate levels of physical activity have around one half the mortality rate of sedentary people who maintain supposedly ideal weight levels." Lest you think these facts have been noticed only by political scientists and law professors, Campos and Oliver draw heavily on the work of biomedical researchers such as Case Western nutritionist Paul Ernsberger, University of Virginia

FAST FACT

A 2006 study published in the scientific journal *Lancet* found that the relationship between waist and hip size is a more useful measure of health risk than body mass index, or BMI, which is a measure of weight relative to height.

physiologist Glenn Gaesser (author of the 1996 book *Big Fat Lies: The Truth About Your Weight and Your Health*), and Steven Blair, the physician/epidemiologist who heads the Dallas-based Cooper Institute.

That's not to say Oliver and Campos don't sometimes overstate their case. "In reality," says Oliver, "we have no clear idea whether any deaths at all can be attributed solely to a person's body weight. "Yet elsewhere he says "there are only two medical conditions that have been shown convincingly to be caused by excess body fat: osteoarthritis of weight-bearing joints and uterine cancer that comes from higher estrogen levels in heavier women." Women do sometimes die from uterine cancer, don't they? And Oliver hedges a bit by mentioning that "fat distribution may actually be a better predictor of mortality than body weight." While "fat on someone's hips and thighs seems to have little or no relationship to the risk of death," he writes, "fat in the belly . . . seems to be problematic."

Oliver also says "about the worst thing that comes from being heavy is that it puts great pressure on people's joints and inhibits their ability to exercise." But if, as Oliver and Campos both suggest, an unreasonable fear of fatness should be blamed for the bad health effects of anorexia, dangerous diet drugs, fluctuating weight, and even smoking ("a common weight loss and weight maintenance strategy," Campos notes), surely obesity can be blamed for deterring the exercise necessary to keep fit. Beyond the fitness issue, at a certain point obesity seriously compromises a person's ability to get around and participate in everyday activities.

Yet none of this contradicts the main scientific point of these two books, which is that the public health establishment, abetted by a credulous and alarmist press, has greatly exaggerated both the strength of the evidence linking fatness to sickness and the level of risk involved. Oliver cites a 2004 *New York Times* story headlined "Death Rate From Obesity Gains Fast on Smoking," based on the highly implausible 400,000-death estimate that was later repudiated by the CDC. He also mentions a 2003 A.P. [Associated Press] article that announced "Obesity at Age 20 Can Cut Life Span by 13 to 20 Years." He notes that "the obesity in question was at a BMI of 45 [305 pounds for an average-height man], which affects less than 1 percent of the population." In a passage that could have been lifted from a critique of U.S. drug policy, Campos says "the basic strategies employed by those who profit from this war are to treat the most extreme cases as typical, to ignore all contrary data, and to recommend 'solutions' that actually cause the problem they supposedly address."

Campos and Oliver emphasize that, while people lose weight all the time (over and over again, in fact), keeping it off over the long term is rare. "Despite a century-long search for a 'cure' for 'overweight,'" says Campos, "we still have no idea how to make fat people thin. "That's a bit of an overstatement, since even Campos concedes that a determined, persistent effort to reduce calorie intake and increase calorie expenditure (an approach he derides as "chronic restrained living") can make fat people thin. But it's true that our bodies resist weight loss, an evolutionary defense against famine that in circumstances of abundance tends to make us chubbier than we might like. Each person seems to be genetically predisposed to a certain weight range. Although it's possible to overcome that predisposition, it requires more effort than most Americans are willing to expend, judging from their flabby guts and quivering thighs. Campos and Oliver say, in essence: Don't bother. Not only is there little evidence that weight loss per se (as opposed to the lifestyle changes that accompany it) improves one's health, but it can be harmful, especially if it involves weight cycling, drugs with dangerous side effects, or radical surgery with high complication rates.

Anti-fat activists such as Yale psychologist Kelly Brownell agree with Campos and Oliver that substantial long-term weight loss is nearly impossible, which is why they emphasize social engineering to change the "food environment" (and the exercise environment), thereby preventing people from getting fat to begin with. Someone who believes fatness itself is not much of a health problem might nevertheless support such policies, most of which are aimed at getting people to eat better (as well as less) and exercise more, goals Campos and Oliver consider worthwhile. Yet Oliver, who agrees with Brownell that the ready availability of cheap, tasty food is the main reason for rising BMIs in the U.S. (because it led to an increase in snacking), is refreshingly skeptical about Brownell's proposal for "junk food" taxes, which he correctly sees as fundamentally unworkable. He likewise dismisses other anti-fat nostrums, including advertising restrictions, bans on soda in schools, and beefed-up physical education, saying none is likely to work. "Getting Americans to really change their eating and exercise patterns would require a level of totalitarianism that would make even Kim Jong Il blush," he writes. "The very rationale of a liberal system such as ours is that individuals are best left to decide for themselves which choices to limit, particularly as long as such decisions do not infringe on the safety or well-being of others."

EVALUATING THE AUTHORS' ARGUMENTS:

Compare the arguments noted by Jacob Sullum against treating obesity as a serious illness with those by the Weight Control Information Network in the previous viewpoint. Does Sullum's article change how you view the information presented by the Weight Control Information Network? Why or why not? Support your reason(s) with evidence from each viewpoint.

Viewpoint

5

Child Obesity Is a Serious Problem

Susan Levine and Rob Stein

"Many of these kids may never escape the corrosive health, psychosocial and economic costs of their obesity."

The problem of child obesity is bad and getting worse, argue Susan Levine and Rob Stein in the following viewpoint. Levine and Stein contend that childhood obesity has become an epidemic, claiming the physiques and health of children all over America. As a result, they say American children now experience disease at higher rates than ever before. Fat children are burdened both physically and emotionally by their condition, argue Levine and Stein. They cannot play or move like normal children and are thus robbed of the activities that make childhood such an exhilarating time; they are socially shunned and depressed as a result of their physical condition; and they are more likely to fail to thrive physically, emotionally, and professionally as adults. For all of these reasons, Levine and Stein conclude that righting America's childhood obesity problem must become a national priority.

Levine and Stein are staff writers for the *Washington Post*, where this viewpoint was originally published.

Susan Levine and Rob Stein, "Obesity Threatens a Generation: 'Catastrophe' of Shorter [Life] Spans, Higher Health Costs," *The Washington Post*, May 17, 2008. Copyright © 2008, *The Washington Post*. Reprinted with permission.

AS YOU READ, CONSIDER THE FOLLOWING QUESTIONS:
   1. What percentage of obese teens do the authors say turn into obese adults?
   2. How much does it cost each year to treat overweight youth, as reported by Levine and Stein?
   3. How many additional cases of coronary heart disease do the authors say the United States is expected to experience by 2035?

An epidemic of obesity is compromising the lives of millions of American children, with burgeoning problems that reveal how much more vulnerable young bodies are to the toxic effects of fat.

In ways only beginning to be understood, being overweight at a young age appears to be far more destructive to well-being than adding excess pounds later in life. Virtually every major organ is at risk. The greater damage is probably irreversible.

A Generation at Risk

Doctors are seeing confirmation of this daily: boys and girls in elementary school suffering from high blood pressure, high cholesterol and painful joint conditions; a soaring incidence of type 2 diabetes, once a rarity in pediatricians' offices; even a spike in child gallstones, also once a singularly adult affliction. Minority youth are most severely affected, because so many are pushing the scales into the most dangerous territory.

With one in three children in this country overweight or worse, the future health and productivity of an entire generation—and a nation—could be in jeopardy.

"There's a huge burden of disease that we can anticipate from the growing obesity in kids," said William H. Dietz, director of the Division of Nutrition, Physical Activity and Obesity at the federal Centers for Disease Control and Prevention. "This is a wave that is just moving through the population."

The trouble is a quarter-century of unprecedented growth in girth. Although the rest of the nation is much heavier, too, among those ages 6 to 19 the rate of obesity has not just doubled, as with their parents and grandparents, but has more than tripled.

Disabled in Their Prime

Because studies indicate that many will never overcome their over-weight—up to 80 percent of obese teens become obese adults—experts fear an exponential increase in heart disease, strokes, cancer and other health problems as the children move into their 20s and beyond. The evidence suggests that these conditions could occur decades sooner and could greatly diminish the quality of their lives. Many could find themselves disabled in what otherwise would be their most productive years.

A Child Obesity Crisis

According to the National Survey of Children's Health (NSCH), childhood overweight and obesity rates for children aged ten to seventeen, defined as a BMI greater than the 85th percentile BMI for age group, ranged from a low of 23.1 percent in Utah and Minnesota to 44.4 percent in Mississippi. Eight of the ten states with the highest rates of overweight and obese children are in the South.

≥ 20% and < 25%   ≥ 30% and < 35%   ≥ 40%

≥ 25% and < 30%   ≥ 35% and < 40%

Taken from: National Survey of Children's Health, 2007.

The cumulative effect could be the country's first generation destined to have a shorter life span than its predecessor. A 2005 analysis by a team of scientists forecast a two- to five-year drop in life expectancy unless aggressive action manages to reverse obesity rates. Since then, children have only gotten fatter.

"Five years might be an underestimate," lead author S. Jay Olshansky of the University of Illinois at Chicago acknowledged recently. . . .

The Growing Expense of Childhood Obesity

The epidemic is expected to add billions of dollars to the U.S. healthcare bill. Treating a child with obesity is three times more costly than treating the average child, according to a study by Thomson Reuters. The research company pegged the country's overall expense of care for overweight youth at $14 billion annually. A substantial portion is for hospital services, since those patients go more frequently to the emergency room [ER] and are two to three times more likely to be admitted.

Given the ominous trend lines, the study concluded, "demand for ER visits, inpatient hospitalizations and outpatient visits is expected to rise dramatically."

Ultimately, the economic calculations will climb higher. No one has yet looked ahead 30 years to project this group's long-term disability and lost earnings, but based on research on the current workforce, which has shown tens of millions of workdays missed annually, indirect costs will also be enormous.

Childhood obesity is nothing less than "a national catastrophe," acting U.S. Surgeon General Steven Galson has declared. The individual toll is equally tragic. "Many of these kids may never escape the corrosive health, psychosocial and economic costs of their obesity," said Risa Lavizzo-Mourey, president of the Robert Wood Johnson Foundation, which has committed at least $500 million over five years to the problem.

Fat from the Start of Life

The cycle of obesity and disease seems to begin before birth: Women who are overweight are more likely to give birth to bigger babies, who are more likely to become obese. "And so you build it up over generations," said Matthew Gillman, associate professor of ambulatory care

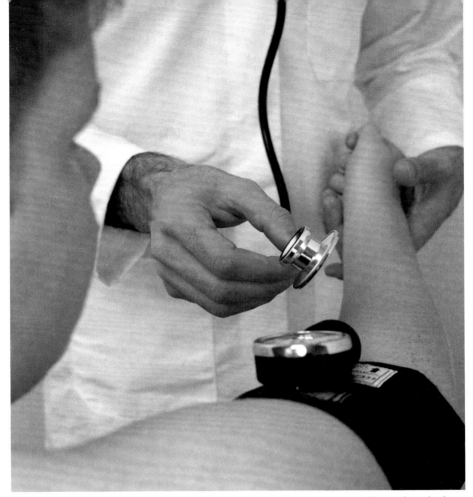

In the United States doctors are seeing more elementary-aged children suffering from high blood pressure, high cholesterol, and painful joint conditions that are caused by obesity.

and prevention at Harvard Medical School. "You get an intergenerational vicious cycle of obesity and disease."

In-utero [before birth] exposure is just part of an exceedingly complex picture. Patterns of eating and activity, often set during early childhood, are influenced by government and education policies, cultural factors and environmental changes. Income and ethnicity are implicated, though these days virtually every community has a problem.

In affluent Loudoun County [Virginia], more than a third of 2- to 5-year-olds are overweight. In some lower-income wards in the District [of Columbia], almost half of all schoolchildren and pre-adolescents fit that label. In middle-class Prince George's County [Maryland], nearly a quarter of all children through age 17 are overweight.

The extra pounds appear to weigh more heavily on bodies that are still forming. Fat cells, researchers have found, pump out a host of hormones and other chemicals that might permanently rewire metabolism.

"A child is not just a little adult. They are still developing and changing. Their systems are still in a process of maturing and being fine-tuned," said David S. Ludwig, an obesity expert at Children's Hospital in Boston. "Being excessively heavy could distort this natural process of growth and development in ways that irreversibly affect the biological pathways."

Robbed of Childhood

As many as 90 percent of overweight children have at least one of a half-dozen avoidable risk factors for heart disease. Even with the most modest increase in future adolescent obesity, a recent study said the United States will face more than 100,000 additional cases of coronary heart disease by 2035.

FAST FACT

According to the American Academy of Child and Adolescent Psychology, between 16 and 33 percent of children and adolescents are obese.

The internal damage does not always take medical testing to diagnose. It is visible as a child laboriously climbs a flight of stairs or tries to sit at a classroom desk, much less rise out of it.

On a playground, obesity exacts a cruel price. "It robs them of their childhood, really," said Melinda S. Sothern of the Louisiana State University Health Sciences Center in New Orleans. "They're robbed of the natural enjoyment of being a kid—being able to play outside, run. If they have high blood pressure, they have a constant risk of stroke."

Physical therapist Brian H. Wrotniak, who works with overweight youth at Children's Hospital of Philadelphia, hears resignation more than anger in his patients' voices. "They complain of simple things like tying their shoes. They can't bend down and tie their shoes because excess fat gets in the way," he said.

Their usual solution: Velcro sneakers.

Being Fat Takes an Emotional Toll

The emotional distress of these ailments, combined with the social stigma of being fat, makes overweight children prone to psychiatric and behavioral troubles. One analysis found that obese youth were seven times more likely to be depressed.

"Obese children are victimized and bullied," said Jeffrey B. Schwimmer, a pediatric gastroenterologist at the University of California at San Diego and Rady Children's Hospital in San Diego. "Not only do other children treat them differently, but teachers treat them differently. And if you look at obese adolescents, their acceptance into college differs. For obese girls, their socioeconomic status is lower. It cuts a broad swath."

Only within this decade, as studies started to corroborate what doctors were seeing firsthand, has child obesity been recognized as a critical public health concern. For the longest time, the signs were all there, in plain view but largely ignored.

Ludwig compares the situation to global warming.

"We don't have all the data yet, but by the time all the data comes in it's going to be too late," he said. "You don't want to see the water rising on the Potomac before deciding global warming is a problem."

> ### EVALUATING THE AUTHORS' ARGUMENTS:
>
> Levine and Stein quote from several sources to support the points they make in their article. Make a list of everyone they quote, including their credentials and the nature of their comments. Then, analyze their sources—are they credible? Are they well qualified to speak on this subject?

The Problem of Child Obesity Has Been Exaggerated

Rob Lyons

> "If fears about obesity are over-stated for adults, they are even more misplaced when it comes to children."

In the following viewpoint Rob Lyons argues that the problem of child obesity has been greatly exaggerated. He examines claims that children who are overweight or obese will be the first generation to live a shorter life than their parents did. Lyons says this claim is highly unlikely and sees no reason to believe it is true. For one, Lyons says overweight children are not likely to turn into overweight adults—the majority of them will lose weight before they enter the prime of their lives. Second, Lyons says that it is unclear that being overweight is a health risk—the deaths of overweight people too often fail to take into account other mitigating factors, such as whether they were poor or smoked. Lyons warns that making overweight children feel that they are sick scars them mentally, which puts them at risk for depression and sadness.

Rob Lyons, "Child Obesity," *spiked-online.com*, March 2, 2006. Copyright © spiked 2006. All rights reserved. Reproduced by permission.

Lyons thinks society should stop casting child obesity as an epidemic and focus instead on making sure children get lots of opportunities to play and feel good about themselves.

AS YOU READ, CONSIDER THE FOLLOWING QUESTIONS:
1. Why does Lyons not recommend that overweight children be encouraged to diet?
2. What does Lyons say is wrong with the assumption that people tend to die from being overweight or obese?
3. By how much does life expectancy rise each decade, according to Lyons?

Panic: A new report by three British official bodies has criticised the government for a lack of progress on tackling child obesity. For example, it has taken 18 months just to agree on how obesity should be measured. The report quotes statistics suggesting that the proportion of obese children has risen from 9.6 per cent in 1995 to 13.7 per cent in 2003. By 2010, the report says that the cost of treating diseases caused by obesity across the whole population—including hypertension [high blood pressure], heart disease and type 2 diabetes—will reach £3.6billion per year. Steve Bundred, chief executive of the Audit Commission, said: 'If the trend continues, this generation will be the first for many decades that doesn't live as long as their parents.'

Don't panic: While it is true that certain diseases are more common in obese adults, the vast majority of people can still expect to live into old age whatever their body shape. If fears about obesity are overstated for adults, they are even more misplaced when it comes to children.

Fat Does Not Last Forever

It is by no means certain that children who are fat will go on to be fat adults. Figures suggest about 30 per cent of obese children stay that heavy in adulthood. Telling a child that being overweight means they are effectively sick may have some impact on their waistlines but is likely to be a recipe for misery in years to come. As Dr Dee

Many experts advocate more play and physical exercise programs, such as the NFL's Play 60 program, as a better way to fight child obesity.

Dawson, a specialist in treating eating disorders, notes: 'We should not be getting children obsessed about what they eat, how much fat and calories there is in their food, how they look. Most of them are perfectly fit and well.'

Nor are the alternatives necessarily much better. While getting some exercise, like walking regularly, seems to be beneficial, taking a lot of exercise may have little additional benefit. Dieting is not only regularly unsuccessful, but has itself been associated with health problems. As an editorial in the *New England Journal of Medicine* noted in 1998, 'Until we have better data about the risks of being overweight and the benefits and risks of losing weight, we should remember that the cure for obesity may be worse than the condition'.

A Highly Unlikely Claim

The most controversial idea, quoted regularly, is that children of this generation will have a lower life expectancy than their parents. While not impossible, it seems highly unlikely. Firstly, it assumes that obesity is the reason that very fat people tend to die younger, rather than lack of exercise, poverty, poor quality of diet or a host of other reasons. Secondly, it suggests that this one lifestyle factor could overcome the effect of all the other medical and social developments which have provided consistent rises in life expectancy. For women, life expectancy has risen every decade for the past 16 decades, and for both sexes lifespans are rising by roughly two years every decade.

If we are really concerned about child obesity, we should stop fretting about what children eat and give them more opportunity for active, independent play. However, given our increasingly risk-averse approach towards kids, there's fat chance of that.

FAST FACT

Data gathered from 1999 to 2006 by the Centers for Disease Control and Prevention reveal that childhood obesity rates have not increased since 1999.

EVALUATING THE AUTHORS' ARGUMENTS:

In this viewpoint Rob Lyons argues that overweight children will be emotionally scarred from being treated as if they are sick. In the previous viewpoint Susan Levine and Rob Stein argue that overweight children will be emotionally scarred from being treated like they are ugly and incapable of doing normal tasks. After reading both viewpoints, which do you think takes the bigger emotional toll on overweight children? Explain your reasoning.

Chapter 2

How Can Obesity Be Prevented?

Many experts say expanding school exercise programs could help prevent obesity. The sporting event pictured here is sponsored by Wellspring Academy, a special school that helps teens and college level students lose weight in addition to offering academic courses.

Viewpoint

1

Posting Nutritional Information in Restaurants Can Prevent Obesity

Ayala Laufer-Cahana

"We deserve easy access to this kind of information that will help us lead healthier lives."

In the following viewpoint Ayala Laufer-Cahana explains why she believes restaurants should be required to post information that details the nutritional content of their foods. She says most people do not realize how many calories are in restaurant food—especially in chain restaurants' dishes and fast food. Giving them the option of seeing the number of calories, grams of fat, and other information when they place their order helps them make healthier choices. Laufer-Cahana says people will eat fewer calories when they are aware of what is in their food, which is good because too many Americans are overweight. In addition, requiring restaurants to post nutritional information will encourage them to create

Ayala Laufer-Cahana, "Calorie Posting Laws Spread—Healthier Choices Follow," *Salon.com*, March 6, 2009. This article first appeared in *Salon.com*, at http://www.salon.com. An online version remains in the Salon archives. Reproduced by permission of the author.

healthier dishes and smaller portions. For all these reasons she says restaurants should post nutritional information near cash registers or on menus and supports legislation that makes this the law.

Laufer-Cahana is a pediatrician who created a line of calorie-free flavored waters as an alternative to sugary, processed drinks.

AS YOU READ, CONSIDER THE FOLLOWING QUESTIONS:
1. What percentage of Subway restaurant patrons saw nutritional information once it was displayed, according to Laufer-Cahana?
2. On average, how many fewer calories does the author say people ate once they were given nutritional information?
3. What changes did Starbucks, Dunkin' Donuts, and McDonald's make to their menus after they were required to post the nutritional content of their foods?

L ast year [in 2008], the Philadelphia City Council passed a measure requiring chain restaurants with more than 15 outlets to disclose calories on menu boards beginning on Jan. 1, 2010. My home town, Philadelphia—famous for the Philly cheese steak, all 900 calories of it—now joins New York City, several counties, and the state of California in passing such a measure.

Why is calorie posting such a good idea?

Ignorance Is Not Nutritional Bliss
1) *Knowing what you're eating is the first step to eating sensibly.*

I believe people will think twice about ordering menu items such as Arby's Sausage Gravy Biscuit (at 960 calories), or McDonald's Vanilla Triple Thick Shake (at 1100 calories), products that supply *half the daily caloric allowance in one meal item.* Until now we could live in ignorant bliss, because unless we went through the trouble of going to the company's website or asking for nutrition charts, we wouldn't know the numbers.

Will consumers lighten up their selections when presented with calorie information? A study published recently in the *American Journal of Public Health* looked at 7,318 customers in 275 fast food restaurants. Of the 11 chains from which food was purchased in this study,

10 did not have calorie information at the point of purchase, and only one—Subway—did. Less than 5% of the study participants saw calorie information when it was provided only in less prominent formats, such as charts on counter mats, distant walls, posters or on a website.

On the other hand, 32% of Subway patrons saw the information, which was displayed *near* the point of purchase. This suggests that laws requiring calorie information be displayed *on menu boards* might increase the proportion of patrons seeing calorie information and taking it into consideration when making their choices.

People Eat Better When They Have Nutritional Information

Among the Subway patrons that reported seeing the caloric information, over a third reported that the information affected their purchase. Objective measurement of calorie content through examination of receipts confirmed that patrons who reported seeing and using calorie information purchased fewer calories than did those reporting they did not see or use calorie information.

While the average caloric reduction amongst the calorie conscious was modest—53 fewer calories—even a modest reduction on a nearly

In July 2009 California became the first state in the country to require chain restaurants to reveal calorie information on their standard menu items.

daily basis for millions of people frequenting fast food venues could be significant in slowing the obesity epidemic. It's estimated that three-quarters of adults use nutrition labels on packaged food, and using labels is associated with eating more healthful diets. There's reason to believe that the same will be true for nutrition information in chain restaurants.

Restaurants Will Make Needed Changes

2) *Companies will be changing their menu items to make their caloric posting more attractive.*

The new measures *encourage companies to reformulate or resize their menu items*, find lower calorie alternatives, and abandon fat and sugar as the secret ingredient that makes all food more palatable. As *New York Times'* Kim Severson writes:

> Restaurants and food companies are lightening recipes and portion sizes. Starbucks, for example, claims to have saved the nation 17 billion calories since last October by swapping 2 percent milk for whole . . . Dunkin' Donuts recently added a low-calorie egg white breakfast sandwich, Cosi is using low-fat mayonnaise and McDonald's large French fries have dropped to 500 calories this year from 570 last year. Quiznos is testing smaller sizes and less-caloric sandwich fillings in its New York stores.
>
> Cathy Nonas of the New York City health department said this is all a reaction to public-health pressure. . . . For some establishments, having their menus exposed by the New York law forced some caloric housecleaning. At Le Pain Quotidien, which has 17 outlets in New York, several items were changed or taken off the menu, said Jack Moran, a vice president. The popular Quiche Lorraine was trimmed to 6 ounces from 11, with extra salad filling out the plate. Sweets like brownies may shrink, too.

FAST FACT

A 2008 poll by Caravan Opinion Research Corporation found that 78 percent of Americans think fast-food and other chain restaurants should list the calories, fat, sugar, or salt content of dishes on their menus.

Customers Need to Know Nutritional Information

Fast-food customers tend to underestimate the calories and fat in the dishes they order. Proponents of menu labeling say it could help people make healthier choices when dining out.

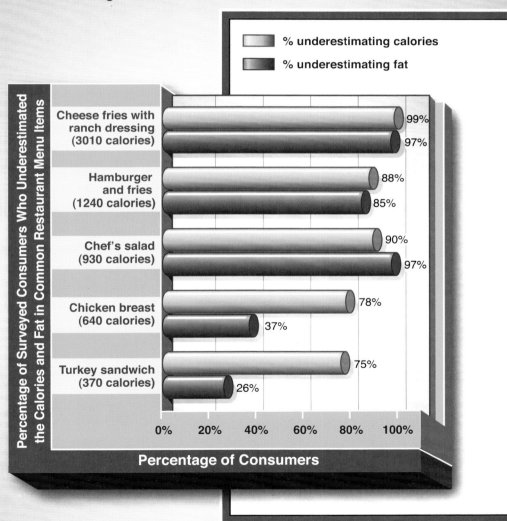

Percentage of Surveyed Consumers Who Underestimated the Calories and Fat in Common Restaurant Menu Items

- % underestimating calories
- % underestimating fat

Cheese fries with ranch dressing (3010 calories): 99% / 97%

Hamburger and fries (1240 calories): 88% / 85%

Chef's salad (930 calories): 90% / 97%

Chicken breast (640 calories): 78% / 37%

Turkey sandwich (370 calories): 75% / 26%

Percentage of Consumers
0% 20% 40% 60% 80% 100%

Taken from: Burton, S., Creyer, E., Kees, J., and Huggins, K., "Attacking the Obesity Epidemic: The Potential Health Benefits of Providing Nutrition Information in Restaurants." *American Journal of Public Health*, 96(9): 1669–1675, September 2006; "Menu Labeling: Does Providing Nutrition Information at the Point of Purchase Affect Consumer Behavior?" Robert Wood Johnson Foundation, June 2009, p. 2.

Americans Have a Right to Know

Now, I believe we should have the freedom to eat whatever we want, no matter how unhealthy and fattening.

On the other hand, I think we have a right to know what's in the food we're buying. The price of our food in calories (and other nutritional information) is sometimes more important than the dollar price.

Restaurants that aren't part of big chains, and don't have standard menus are not subject to these laws, and I think that's fine; it would be too costly to provide nutritional data on changing menus for these small businesses. I also think that eating at these kinds of restaurants is not an everyday thing for most people.

Since I eat most of my meals at home, I'm not concerned by the richness of the food my family eats when we go out to dine once every few weeks. We enjoy it as a special treat. I assume that the meal is indulgent in its use of ingredients that I try to use less of at home, and in these occasions, I just don't worry about the calories.

On the other hand, if people are eating out *regularly*, as people often do at the fast food eateries (the average American eats out *four* meals a week), caloric information becomes important. Since the nutritional information exists anyway, putting it where it can be seen *before* selections are made, thus making consumers more informed, is an incredibly useful practice.

I hope these menu labeling bills will build momentum for national legislation, making menu labeling the law everywhere people are eating fast food. We deserve easy access to this kind of information that will help us lead healthier lives.

EVALUATING THE AUTHOR'S ARGUMENTS:

Laufer-Cahana argues that people eat fewer calories once they become aware of the nutritional content of their food. Think about some of the fast-food dishes you eat. Would finding out that they have 150 more calories than you thought cause you to change your order? Why or why not?

Viewpoint 2

Restaurants Should Not Have to Post Nutritional Information

"Is it really the job of the state to coerce restaurants into confronting diners with information most of them aren't interested in?"

Jeff Jacoby

The government should not require restaurants to post nutritional information, argues Jeff Jacoby in the following viewpoint. Jacoby contends that such legislation is unnecessary because fast-food customers do not want to know the nutritional content of their food. He says customers already ignore the nutritional information that comes on packaged foods, and there is no reason to think they would pay attention to such information if it were listed on a menu. Jacoby considers efforts to make menu labeling the law to be an affront to personal liberty—in his opinion, both restaurants and patrons should be able to do what they want without being forced by the government. Jacoby concludes that since people will ignore most nutritional postings, laws that mandate them will not reduce obesity. He warns they will only reduce freedom and expand the power of the state.

Jeff Jacoby, "Want a Warning Label with Those Fries?" *The Boston Globe*, January 11, 2009. Reproduced by permission.

Jacoby is a columnist for the *Boston Globe*, where this article was originally published.

AS YOU READ, CONSIDER THE FOLLOWING QUESTIONS:
1. What was the finding of a 2006 study at the University of Vermont? What bearing does it have on Jacoby's argument?
2. In what way does Jacoby say the state is trying to make fast food like tobacco, global warming, or cars without airbags?
3. What does Jacoby mean when he warns of a "government-approved body mass index"?

The worthies who govern Massachusetts haven't been able to keep the state's population from dwindling, its property taxes from soaring, its budget from imploding, its Big Dig [Boston tunnel system] from leaking, or its politicians from getting arrested. But failure hasn't diminished their ambition—or their presumption: Now they're going to keep the rest of us from overeating.

People Do Not Care About What's in Their Food

On Thursday [January 8, 2009], Governor Deval Patrick's administration launched Mass in Motion, a new war on obesity that it calls "the most comprehensive effort to date to address the serious problem of overweight and obesity in the Commonwealth." Already up and running is a shiny new website, which appears to consist mostly of trite exhortations to eat sensibly and do more exercise. Needless to say, the administration plans to spend money on its crusade, current budget straits notwithstanding. After all, if the state doesn't pump $750,000 into such "wellness initiatives" as "expanding the availability of farmers' markets" and designing "transportation systems that encourage walking," who will?

But the heart of the new campaign, as with most government initiatives, is coercion. Following the lead of California, New York City, and Seattle, Massachusetts officials plan to compel restaurant chains to conspicuously post the calorie content of all their offerings, either on the menu or at the counter. Obesity warriors want restaurants to be forced to publicize the nutritional content of the foods they sell so that consumers can make a reasoned decision about what to eat. "People often really are not aware of what's sitting on their plate," the director of Boston Medical Center's nutrition and weight management program, Dr. Caroline Apovian, told *The Boston Globe*. "But if the information is sitting right in front of you . . . it's hard to deny."

Actually, not that hard. When it comes to nutrition as to so much else, human beings are quite adept at denying, ignoring, or discounting information they would rather not deal with. A 2006 study by researchers at the University of Vermont found that the more often one eats in fast-food restaurants, the less likely he is to pay attention

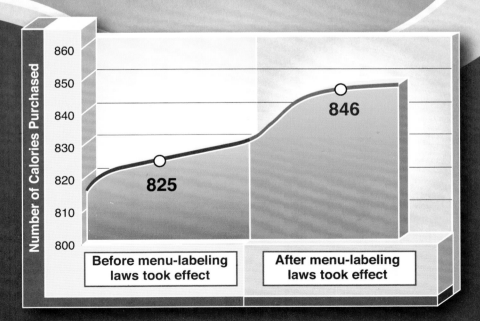

Calorie Postings Will Not Reduce Obesity

A study of food purchases made in New York City after menu-labeling laws went into effect found that the mean number of calories purchased actually increased. Although 50 percent of study participants said they noticed the information, just 28 percent said it positively affected their purchases.

Number of Calories Purchased

860
850
840
830
820
810
800

825

846

Before menu-labeling laws took effect

After menu-labeling laws took effect

Taken from: Thomas A. Farley et. al. "New York City's Fight over Calorie Labeling," *Health Affairs*, vol. 28, no. 6, November/December, 2009. pp. 1098–1109.

to food labels. "These . . . data suggest," they concluded, that "recent legislation advocating for greater labeling of restaurant food may not be particularly effective."

A Threat to Freedom

Is it really the job of the state to coerce restaurants into confronting diners with information most of them aren't interested in? The food-service industry is exceptionally competitive and highly sensitive to customer preferences; if enough diners wanted to look at obtrusive calorie charts when eating out, restaurants would already be providing them. Jacob Sullum of *Reason* magazine puts his finger on it: "A legal requirement is necessary not because diners want conspicuous nutritional information but because, by and large, they *don't* want it."

Nanny-statists [a negative term for those who encourage government intervention on behalf of its citizens] find it easy to disregard consumers' wishes. After all, they reason, it's for their own good—obesity is a deadly scourge that government must not ignore. Massachusetts Public Health Commissioner John Auerbach warned darkly last week that "unless we make progress"—that is, unless the government imposes new restrictions on liberty—"overweight and obesity will overtake smoking as the leading cause of preventable death in Massachusetts."

That always seems to be the nannies' bottom line, whether the risk is said to be from tobacco, global warming, or cars without airbags: We must take away some freedom or more people will die.

> **FAST FACT**
>
> A 2009 study published in the journal *Health Affairs* found that only about half the customers at New York City fast-food restaurants noticed calorie postings after a law there made such labeling mandatory. Of those people, less than 30 percent said the information influenced their order.

Postings Will Not Reduce Obesity

But what will the government do when mandatory calorie information in chain restaurants doesn't make a dent in obesity rates? Extend

Whether forcing restaurants to post nutritional information will improve Americans' eating choices is a matter of debate.

the mandate to all restaurants regardless of size? To supermarket display shelves and freezer sections? Will warning labels be required on packages of Oreo cookies and Oscar Mayer hot dogs? Will new regulations prohibit fast-food restaurants and confectioners from running ads on TV or in magazines? And if our collective waistline *still* doesn't shrink, will the most fattening foods be permitted only to consumers with a government-approved body-mass index? Or simply banned altogether?

For at least 30 years, the food industry has been labeling packaged foods with nutritional information; with the rise of the Internet, Americans have access to more such information today than ever before. Yet Americans are also fatter than ever before.

Hectoring people about calories doesn't usually make them thinner. It doesn't work when family members do it. It won't work any better when regulators do it. Not even in Massachusetts.

EVALUATING THE AUTHOR'S ARGUMENTS:

Jacoby argues that since customers do not want to know nutritional information, there is no need to create laws that make sure they have it. What do you think? Should laws be based on what the public wants or based on what is good for them? Explain your reasoning and include quotes from the texts you have read in your answer.

Viewpoint

3

Requiring Schools to Offer Physical Education Classes Can Combat Obesity in Children

"PE is at the core of promoting healthy choices."

Bryan McCullick

In the following viewpoint Bryan McCullick argues that implementing and improving physical education programs can reduce and prevent obesity. McCullick explains that very few schools require students to take PE classes, and most have insufficient or over-crowded athletic spaces and materials. But athletic activity is important for losing weight, staying fit, eating well, and cultivating other healthy habits that are critical for young people. McCullick suggests schools institute not just PE classes but recess, intramural sports

Bryan McCullick, "Obesity Won't Improve Without Reforming PE," *Atlanta Journal-Constitution*, December 9, 2009. Copyright © 2010 *The Atlanta Journal-Constitution*. Republished with permission of *The Atlanta Journal-Constitution*, conveyed through Copyright Clearance Center, Inc.

and clubs, interscholastic sports, and opportunities for students to walk and bike to school. McCullick says instituting this kind of comprehensive physical education is an inexpensive way to combat an expensive problem; he says obesity-related problems rack up billions in heath care and economic costs, most of which could be avoided if Americans were taught to be physically active at a young age. He concludes that school-mandated physical education should be part of health care reform in America.

McCullick is an associate professor of physical education in the University of Georgia's College of Education and is research coordinator for the National Association for Sport and Physical Education.

AS YOU READ, CONSIDER THE FOLLOWING QUESTIONS:
1. How much money does McCullick say could be saved by improving physical activity rates by just 5 percent over a five-year period?
2. What percentage of high schools require phys ed programs? What percentage of elementary schools?
3. What percentage of parents think phys ed should be required? What percentage of teachers?

O besity-related health care costs in the United States for one year—2008—were an estimated $147 billion, according to a recent Centers for Disease Control study. That's nearly a quarter of what the latest health care reform proposal will cost over the next 10 years.

It seems clear that reforming the amount and quality of school-based physical education [PE] programs is fundamental to improving America's health care. Yet, this idea is conspicuously absent from the health care debate as overweight and obesity among both adults and youth reach epidemic proportions.

Schools Are Obligated to Care for Students' Health
If schools are places where responsible citizenship is fostered, they should also have an obligation to help children develop the skills, knowledge and confidence necessary to maintain a healthy lifestyle that can prevent or reduce costly future health care.

PE is at the core of promoting healthy choices. A comprehensive school program includes PE, health education, healthy food options, recess for elementary school students, intramural sport programs and physical activity clubs, and interscholastic sports for high school students. Ideally, schools would also include physical activity breaks, walk/bike to school programs, appropriate physical activity in after-school child care programs, and staff wellness programs.

Students participate in a physical education program at a Chicago school. Because the gym doubles as the school cafeteria, the number of hours it can be used for physical education is limited.

While preventative health care measures have been included in the [Barack] Obama administration's proposals, none include school-based PE reform. When will health care reform focus on what should be done to prevent obesity-related illnesses?

Fitter Children Save Money

A 2009 report from the California Center for Public Health Advocacy on the annual economic costs of physical inactivity, obesity and being overweight in California estimated that in 2006 physical inactivity cost $20.19 billion, being overweight and obesity $20.98 billion. That's more than $41 billion in economic costs for Californians alone.

The preponderance of these costs were shouldered by the public and private employers in the form of health insurance and lost productivity, the report said. But an estimated $612 billion could be saved by improving physical activity rates and healthy weight maintenance by only 5 percent over five years.

A seemingly simple solution, yes, but one that is missing a crucial component: People must learn how to move, value physical activity, make good food choices and avoid risky behavior. While this might occur outside of schools, improving school-based PE will increase the potential for American youth to learn and apply this information now and later, as adults.

Improving prevention measures such as PE is certainly cheaper than treating disease. Properly funded, supported and utilized, health-related PE is a nearly universal means to increase physical activity, curtail obesity rates and decrease the numbers of people who suffer from the multitude of diseases and lifelong health problems linked to obesity. While some say PE has no proven effect on children's health or long-term activity patterns, there is evidence clearly linking increased physical activity to lower disease risk.

A Shocking Lack of PE

The National Association for Sport and Physical Education's 2006 "Shape of the Nation Report" shows shocking underuse of PE by most states in the U.S. Only 8 percent of elementary schools, 6.4 percent of middle/junior high schools and 5.8 percent of high schools require daily PE. In spite of data revealing that 85 percent of parents and 81 percent of

Food Portions Have Been Super-Sized

Portion size has grown substantially in the last twenty years—this has had a significant impact in the number of calories consumed and could in part explain the rise in obesity rates among children.

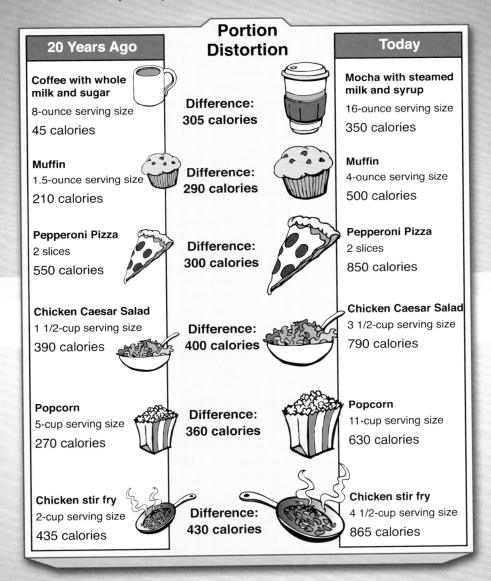

Portion Distortion

20 Years Ago

Coffee with whole milk and sugar

8-ounce serving size

45 calories

Muffin

1.5-ounce serving size

210 calories

Pepperoni Pizza

2 slices

550 calories

Chicken Caesar Salad

1 1/2-cup serving size

390 calories

Popcorn

5-cup serving size

270 calories

Chicken stir fry

2-cup serving size

435 calories

Today

Mocha with steamed milk and syrup

16-ounce serving size

350 calories

Muffin

4-ounce serving size

500 calories

Pepperoni Pizza

2 slices

850 calories

Chicken Caesar Salad

3 1/2-cup serving size

790 calories

Popcorn

11-cup serving size

630 calories

Chicken stir fry

4 1/2-cup serving size

865 calories

Difference: 305 calories

Difference: 290 calories

Difference: 300 calories

Difference: 400 calories

Difference: 360 calories

Difference: 430 calories

Taken from: National Heart, Lung and Blood Institute Obesity Initiative, Portion Distortion II Interactive Quiz. http://hp2010.nhlbihin.net/portion.index.htm. Also see Young, L. R., and M. Nestle, "The Contributions of Expanding Portion Sizes to the U.S. Obesity Epidemic." *American Journal of Public Health* 92, no. 2 (2002): 246–249. Obtained from Trust for America's Health, "F as in Fat: How Obesity Policies Are Failing in America," Robert Wood Johnson Foundation, 2009, p. 28.

teachers believe that students should be required to take PE every day at every grade level, such programs are nonexistent in many places.

Think your child is getting the physical education he or she needs? Consider this: The Georgia state rule for the amount of health and physical education elementary students are to receive is 90 hours per year. Ask your child how many times a week he or she attends a PE or health class and calculate the time for the year. Many area schools allow for only 60 minutes of physical education a week. Over a 36-week school year that translates to only 36 hours per year—54 hours less than what the state recommends.

Some would claim the shortage is due to an "unfunded mandate" but that claim is misused. The real culprit is the emphasis on federal and state pressure for high-stakes testing and the impact those results have on teachers' jobs and salaries.

Total PE Reform Is Needed

However, increasing the amount of PE alone is not the solution. The quality of PE students' need is glaringly omitted in anyone's talking points in the health care debate. Overcrowded gymnasiums, insufficient or outdated resources, and sometimes inhumane working conditions (no air conditioning in gyms when school begins in August) are archetypal for many PE programs.

Further, 33 percent of states reacting, again, to federal mandates for "highly qualified" teachers have relaxed licensure requirements for PE teachers. To help young people develop into physically educated individuals, a specialist with a body of knowledge and skills is needed in every school. The days of the ball-rolling, coffee-swilling, game-prepping PE "coach" have contributed to the current obesity rate increase.

> **FAST FACT**
>
> The Centers for Disease Control and Prevention report that just 3.8 percent of elementary, 7.9 percent of middle, and 2.1 percent of high schools provide daily physical education. Twenty-two percent of schools do not require students to take any physical education at all.

Unlike any of the current proposals from those engaged in the health care reform debate, this is one solution with financial and preventative health ramifications that would actually benefit all involved, especially children. Given the dramatic rise of childhood obesity, the associated health consequences and derivative costs of obesity have also steadily risen. Failing to address school-based PE reform as a high priority item in health care reform is at best, ignorant, and at worst, societal suicide.

EVALUATING THE AUTHOR'S ARGUMENTS:

McCullick suggests schools implement comprehensive physical education programs that would consist of gym and health classes, healthy food options, recess, intramural sports and clubs, interscholastic sports, and more. Which, if any, of these programs are available at your school? Do you think they make important differences in the fight against obesity, as McCullick suggests they will? Why or why not?

Viewpoint
4

Schools Should Not Be Required to Offer Physical Education Classes

Jay Matthews

"I know we haven't finished that chapter yet, kids, but hey, it's time for push-ups."

In the following viewpoint Jay Matthews argues that schools should not be required to offer physical education (PE) classes to their students. He discusses a proposal that would make it mandatory for students to get at least thirty to forty-five minutes of physical education a day. Matthews says the proposed law is well-meaning but fails to take into account the fact that the school day is barely long enough to cover academics.

He thinks it is wrong to reduce class time—which many schools are short on to begin with—to increase physical education because physical activity, unlike academic learning and achievement, is something students can do on their own after school. Matthews says it might be acceptable to

Jay Matthews, "More Required PE—a Bad Idea from Good People," *The Washington Post*, December 27, 2009. Copyright © 2009, *The Washington Post*. Reprinted with permission.

make PE mandatory if school officials are willing to lengthen the school day to include it. But until that happens, it is wrong to take away from students' already strapped academic time.

Matthews writes an education blog for the *Washington Post*.

AS YOU READ, CONSIDER THE FOLLOWING QUESTIONS:
1. What are the current PE requirements for students in the D.C. area, according to Matthews?
2. How much time does Matthews say students have each school day to work on academics?
3. Adding how much time to each school day does Matthews say would make him cheer?

Sometimes it is the smartest, most concerned policymakers who do the most harm to schools. My favorite recent example is the Healthy Schools Act, a bill introduced by D.C. council member Mary M. Cheh and Council Chairman Vincent C. Gray two weeks ago [in December 2009].

"One of the Dumbest Ideas"

Cheh and Gray are good people trying to address a national epidemic of childhood obesity and insufficient physical activity. In Cheh's press release she notes that 18 percent of D.C. high school students are obese, 70 percent fail to meet the U.S. Centers for Disease Control recommended levels of physical activity and 84 percent do not attend physical education classes daily. It is their solution that troubles me.

FAST FACT

According to the National Conference of State Legislatures, eighteen states have minimum time or frequency requirements for physical education classes for at least some grades. Just two states, New York and Illinois, have minimum time or frequency PE requirements for all grades.

I am unqualified to comment on the food parts of the bill. I have never written about nutrition. I would be embarrassed to reveal the amount of crackers, cookies and ice cream I eat each day. I can only wonder how D.C. will pay for the required fresh produce from local growers in all schools, and how they will get students to eat it.

The bill's physical education requirements are its worst part—a nifty-sounding reform that many of the District's best principals and teachers will declare one of the dumbest ideas they ever heard.

First Lady Michelle Obama and Mexico's Frst Lady, Margarita Zavala, participate in a physical education class at a local Washington, D.C., school. Many schools have limited their physical education programs due to budget cuts.

Mandated Physical Education Is Wrong

At the moment, D.C. students from kindergarten through eighth grade have two P.E. periods a week of 45 minutes each. High-schoolers need just a semester and a half of a similar P.E. regime to graduate. The new bill would require every public school student in kindergarten through fifth grade to have 150 minutes of P.E. (30 minutes a day). Sixth- through eighth-graders would be required to take 225 minutes (45 a day).

Why shouldn't our kids get more exercise? In a perfect world, that would be a lovely idea. But the D.C. schools are in crisis. We no longer have, the latest federal figures show, children with the lowest test scores in urban America. But even with recent gains we are still far below average, and not that far ahead of Detroit, which has supplanted us at the bottom of the list.

Students Need School Time to Learn

Nowhere in her press release does Cheh address the key issue—the fact that the D.C. schools need to do a better job using the limited time they have, about six and a half hours a day, to address students' weaknesses in reading, writing, math, science and social studies. She and Gray are telling teachers trying to turn around those poor performances that now they will have even less time to do it.

I know we haven't finished that chapter yet, kids, but hey, it's time for push-ups.

If Cheh were saying we should add an hour to the school day of every child, and use half of that new time for more exercise, I would cheer. Many of the city's most successful public schools are charters that have used their independence from district rules to give children eight or nine hours of learning each day.

Politicians Must Consider the Consequences

The Healthy Schools Act says nothing about longer school days. It goes one bad step further by depriving those charters of their freedom to make their own decisions. If the bill passes, they also will have to adhere to the rule that mandates 30 to 45 minutes of P.E. a day. (The bill includes a possible exemption for charter schools that don't have space for P.E., but that's not the issue.)

Cheh says she is open to changes. The D.C. schools that work best are run by principals who have the power to teach their students any way they and their teachers think best, as long as achievement improves. Many of them may find a 45-minute daily P.E. period just what they need to energize their students.

But telling them they have to do it whether it works for them or not is a bad idea, one of many from politicians who thought they were doing the right thing but never considered the consequences.

EVALUATING THE AUTHORS' ARGUMENTS:

Matthews argues that forcing schools to offer more physical education takes away from students' time to work on academics. How do you think Bryan McCullick, author of the previous viewpoint, would respond to this argument? After reading both authors' perspectives, with which one do you ultimately agree on the matter? List at least two pieces of evidence that swayed you.

Schools Should Send Home Weight-Loss Report Cards

Jill Zeman

"A lot of positive things have come out of those letters."

In the following viewpoint Jill Zeman reports on an Arkansas program in which out-of-shape students are sent home with weight-loss report cards. The cards record each child's body-mass index and state whether the child has been judged to be overweight or obese. Although the weight-loss report cards were initially unpopular among parents, almost all took action to make their children healthier. Zeman says parents took their overweight children to the doctor, enrolled them in fitness classes, cooked healthier dishes for them, and cut sweets out of their diet. As a result, the weight-loss report cards have helped not only the overweight child look and feel better, but have also helped his or her whole family adopt healthier habits. For all of these reasons Zeman reports that weight-loss report cards are a good solution to improving the problem of childhood obesity.

Zeman is a journalist who writes articles for the Associated Press.

Jill Zeman, "Arkansas Policy of Weighing Kids Leads to Better Health," The Associated Press, June 2, 2006. Reprinted with permission of The Associated Press.

AS YOU READ, CONSIDER THE FOLLOWING QUESTIONS:
  1. What happened to fitness-class attendance and diet-pill use when weight-loss report cards began being sent home with overweight students, according to Zeman?
  2. What year did Arkansas schools start sending home weight-loss report cards?
  3. What percentage of parents does Zeman say approve of Arkansas' weigh-in program? What percentage of adolescents?

It's been two years since Arkansas schools started sending letters home to parents with their children's report cards — letters telling them if their kids were fat.

Plenty of parents weren't happy. But a lot of them did something about it.

Letters Have Changed Lifestyles

Suddenly there were more visits to the pediatrician for talks about weight problems. Fitness-class attendance is up. Diet-pill use by high schoolers is down.

And more states are following Arkansas' lead, including California, Florida and Pennsylvania, which have adopted similar programs.

Dr. Karen Young, medical director for the pediatric fitness clinic at Arkansas Children's Hospital, told of a mother upset when she got word from school that her child was overweight. The mother wanted a second opinion from Young, but in the meantime, she cut sweets from the family diet and slimmed the child down before the appointment.

"Even though she was upset with the letter and felt it was wrong, she still changed the family's lifestyle," Young said. "A lot of positive things have come out of those letters."

Good for the Whole Family

The letters record each child's body-mass index, the same weight-height formula used to calculate adult obesity. The first batch went out in the 2003–04 school year.

Across the state 57 percent of doctors said they had at least one parent bring in their child's letter from the school for discussion during the last school year.

Young said she's had more visits from parents seeking help for the entire family.

"I don't care what size their siblings are or their parents, everyone in the family should eat healthy and exercise," she said. "What's good for them is good for everybody."

Child Obesity on the Rise

Nationwide, about 17 percent of school-aged children are obese and 32 percent are overweight. Some believe sending home weight-loss report cards can make families more aware of their child's physical status and help him or her improve it.

NH 12.8%
VT 12.9%
ME 12.9%
MA 12.9%
WA 11.1%
RI 12.9%
NY 17.1%
CT 12.9%
OR 9.6%
MT 11.8%
ND 11.4%
MN 13.1%
MI 12.4%
PA 15.0%
NJ 12.9%
ID 11.8%
WI
WY 10.2%
SD 13.2%
IA 11.2%
IL 20.7%
IN 14.6%
OH 18.5%
WV 18.9%
VA 15.2%
DE 12.9%
NV 15.2%
UT 11.4%
CO 14.2%
NE 15.8%
MD 12.9%
CA 15.0%
KS 16.2%
MO 13.6%
KY 20.6%
TN 15.3%
NC 18.6%
SC
AZ 17.8%
NM 16.0%
OK 16.4%
AR 21.9%
MS
AL 17.9%
GA 21.3%
TX 20.4%
LA 20.7%
FL 18.3%
AK 14.1%
HI 11.2%

Proportion of obese children increased since 2003
Decreased since 2003

Note: Obesity classification is based on children's body mass index for their age. Children in the top 5 percent on growth charts were considered obese. Data: National Opinion Research Center.

Taken from: Centers for Disease Control and Prevention and *Wall Street Journal*, July 20, 2009.

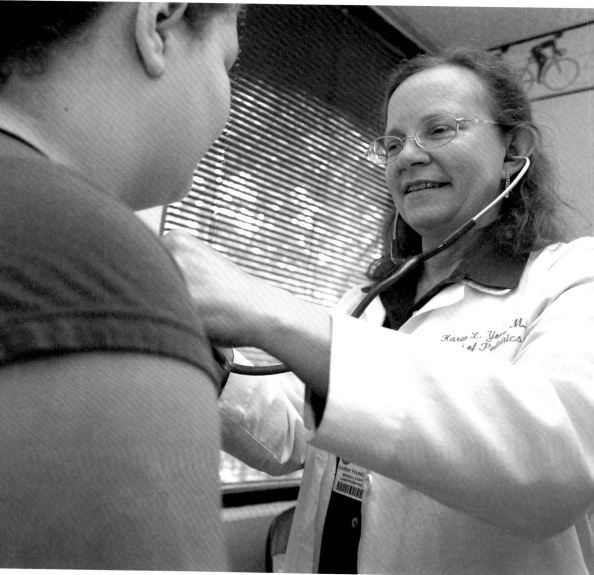

Dr. Karen Young of the Arkansas Children's Hospital clinic examines a student as part of the nation's first obesity testing for public school students.

More Self-Esteem

A Local TV news report on Young's clinic led Marsha Simon-Younger to enroll her 11-year-old daughter Nasirah in fitness classes. Since Nasirah joined this spring, she's felt better and is eating healthier, her mother said.

"At first, my daughter was really reluctant to go because she thought of it as a fat camp," said Simon-Younger. But once Nasirah arrived, she saw a friend from church and Girl Scouts and felt at ease.

"She has more self-esteem," and she tries different foods, the mother said. "Sometimes we might fall off the wagon, but we get right back on."

And the state has found that most parents and children are comfortable with the weigh-in program—71 percent of parents and 61 percent of adolescents, according to a survey.

"Once they realized we didn't hand (the letters) to kids to wave around the schoolyard . . . a lot of the original concerns were alleviated," said Gov. Mike Huckabee, who has championed healthy diets after dropping more than 100 pounds himself. "This was not an invasive procedure where a child is asked to lift a shirt and be pinched with calipers [to measure body fat]."

FAST FACT

Each year, the University of Baltimore Obesity Initiative grades states on their efforts to reduce obesity in children. In 2007, for the first time, six states—California, Illinois, Oklahoma, Pennsylvania, South Carolina, and Tennessee—received "A" grades for their efforts, which included measuring and reporting students' body mass index (BMI) profiles.

EVALUATING THE AUTHORS' ARGUMENTS:

In this viewpoint Zeman reports on the positive changes that took place after students were sent home with weight-loss report cards. In the following viewpoint, J. Justin Wilson disagrees that positive changes are likely to take place as a result of weight-loss report cards. After reading both viewpoints, with which perspective do you agree? Why? List at least two pieces of evidence that helped you form your opinion.

Schools Should Not Send Home Weight-Loss Report Cards

"Report cards don't work. It doesn't take a report card to tell parents that their child is overweight; it takes two eyes."

J. Justin Wilson

In the following viewpoint J. Justin Wilson argues that sending home weight-loss report cards is not a good way to get overweight students to lose weight. He explains that weight-loss report cards are based on body mass index (BMI), which is a flawed way to determine whether or not someone is overweight or obese. Furthermore, he argues that sending home such cards only shames those students, making them feel self-conscious and bad about their bodies. A more positive way to help overweight kids lose weight, says Wilson, is to add physical education to the school day. He thinks extending recess, adding gym classes, and incorporating exercise into class projects is a more positive and productive way to approach the problem of child obesity. He concludes that schools should not send home weight-loss report cards because they

J. Justin Wilson, "BMI 'Report Cards' Won't Keep Kids Healthy," *The MetroWest Daily News*, May 29, 2009. Copyright © 2009 *The MetroWest Daily News*. Some rights reserved. Reproduced by permission of the author.

neither accurately identify overweight students nor help students to lose weight.

Wilson is a senior research analyst at the Center for Consumer Freedom, a nonprofit coalition supported by restaurants, food companies, and consumers that promotes personal responsibility and consumer choice.

AS YOU READ, CONSIDER THE FOLLOWING QUESTIONS:
1. What percentage of parents said their kids were humiliated by the weight-loss report card system, according to Wilson?
2. How long is recess in elementary schools in Peabody, Massachusetts, according to the author?
3. What percentage of Massachusetts high school students does Wilson say do not take a daily gym class?

In the campaign to eradicate childhood obesity, schools around the country have banned everything from birthday treats to vending machines. But when it comes to slimming down students, the so-called food police aren't making much progress.

Now the Massachusetts Public Health Council has decided to take another approach: Body Mass Index [BMI] surveillance. The new program will monitor kids' BMI, and parents of heavy children will be notified with a special "report card."

Sadly, this scheme won't encourage healthy habits any more than turning cupcakes into contraband [a forbidden good]. But there is a better way. If Massachusetts officials are committed to helping students lose weight, they need to get kids moving.

BMI Is a Poor Measure of Who Needs Help

The first problem with measuring students' BMI is that it's a poor measure of who's actually overweight or obese. The BMI is a simple ratio of height to weight, used by governments to classify people as "normal," "overweight," or "obese." The result is a system so flawed that it considers [football player] Tom Brady officially fat. (It doesn't take muscle mass and fat mass into account.)

Even the Centers for Disease Control and Prevention [CDC] openly doubts the effectiveness of BMI as a health promotion tool.

NutritionFacts

Nutrition Facts	
Total Fat	50%
Sugar	50%
Shot at Diabetes	100%
Heart Disease odds	100%
Parental responsibility	0%
Personal responsibility	0%

MICHELLE OBAMA ANNOUNCES STRATEGY TO COMBAT CHILDHOOD OBESITY IN AMERICA: INGREDIENTS LABELS WILL NOW BE PRINTED ON OUR CHILDREN.

(c) 2010 David Fitzsimmons, *The Arizona Star*, and PoliticalCartoons.com.

Report Card Programs Fail

Though this so-called surveillance system is new to Massachusetts, the Bay State isn't the first to experiment with it. With the intention of tackling its own obesity problem, Arkansas introduced a similar "report card" program in 2003. It failed miserably.

As *The Baltimore Sun* reported three years later, "The BMI testing has not put a dent in the state's number of overweight kids." Thirteen percent of parents reported that the program was a source of humiliation for their kids at school.

Instead of finding innovative ways to lower children's self esteem, schools should look at what researchers have discovered about weight gain among teens and 'tweens: It has little to do with BMI measurements, or even junk food.

More Physical Activity Works Better than Report Cards

Research published in February [2009] in the journal *Pediatrics* found that nearly a third of schoolchildren get little or no daily recess. The study's authors suggest that childhood obesity should be attacked with more physical activity in school, where kids spend a majority of their waking hours.

The *Pediatrics* study also found that children who are allotted recess time in school behave better in class. And a month earlier, Harvard researchers demonstrated a clear relationship between physical fitness and academic achievement.

Compare that with the measly 10-minute recess at Peabody elementary schools, for instance. (That's about how long it takes to pick teams for kickball.)

Lack of exercise is a problem that continues as students grow older. According to a 2007 CDC survey, 82 percent of Massachusetts high school students didn't have daily gym class. Yet 28 percent watched three or more hours of TV on school days.

In a speech at the National Food Policy Conference in 2003, then-FDA [Food and Drug Administration] Commissioner Dr. Mark McClellan said that "in a debate that has often focused on foods alone, actual levels of caloric intake among the young haven't appreciably changed over the last 20 years."

A Positive Approach Is Needed

Rather than demonize birthday goodies or scold the parents of overweight kids, shouldn't teachers be looking for a positive approach to help students manage their weight?

The difficulty is that feel-good legislation like Massachusetts BMI reports cards is easy but ineffective. Getting kids to move is a much more difficult task for legislators to accomplish, though it is possible.

Teachers at Mars Hill Elementary School in North Carolina are already leading the way by taking an "exercise first" approach to fighting childhood obesity. Their third-graders have nearly enough miles on their odometers to have walked across the state and back.

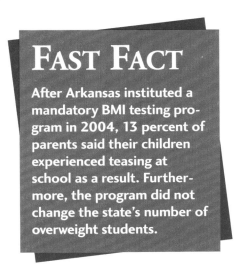

FAST FACT

After Arkansas instituted a mandatory BMI testing program in 2004, 13 percent of parents said their children experienced teasing at school as a result. Furthermore, the program did not change the state's number of overweight students.

BMI report cards don't work. It doesn't take a report card to tell parents that their child is overweight; it takes two eyes. Massachusetts officials should employ methods that are known to help fight childhood obesity. It's time to teach children healthy habits and give them enough time to do what they do best: play.

EVALUATING THE AUTHORS' ARGUMENTS:

J. Justin Wilson argues that weight-loss report cards make students feel ashamed and embarrassed. In the previous viewpoint Jill Zeman reports that weight-loss report cards initially evoke feelings of shame and embarrassment, but these feelings inspired parents and students to make healthy lifestyle changes. What do you think? Are weight-loss report cards a good tool for motivating families to change their behavior? Or do they just make students and parents feel bad about themselves?

Chapter 3

What Role Should the Government Play in Fighting Obesity?

First Lady Michelle Obama addresses students at a Jackson, Mississippi, public school about her "Let's Move" program to fight childhood obesity and promote healthy life styles.

Viewpoint 1

The Government Should Play a Leading Role in Helping People Lose Weight

"The serious health risks of obesity, combined with rapidly rising obesity-related health care costs, warrant not only public attention but also public action and spending."

Ron Haskins, Christina Paxson, and Elisabeth Donahue

In the following viewpoint Ron Haskins, Christina Paxson, and Elisabeth Donahue argue that the government is responsible for helping its citizens lose weight and fight obesity. They argue that government intervention is needed because obesity has become a public health crisis that costs the government billions of dollars per year to treat. As such, it is in the government's interest to reduce these costs. Another reason the government should help fight obesity is because much of the problem lies with America's youth, a segment of the population the authors say the

Ron Haskins, Christina Paxson, and Elisabeth Donahue, excerpted from *The Future of Children, Policy Brief.* Washington, DC: Princeton-Brookings, 2006. Copyright © 2006 Brookings Institution. Reproduced by permission.

government is in a unique position to help. They argue that children become obese because of junk food advertising and because of a lack of good food and exercise options at school—the government is in charge of both regulating such advertising and making changes to school lunch and exercise programs. The authors conclude that fighting obesity is a huge challenge, one that cannot be met without the help of various branches of government.

Haskins, Paxson, and Donahue are editors of the *Future of Children*, a journal published jointly by Princeton University and the Brookings Institution.

AS YOU READ, CONSIDER THE FOLLOWING QUESTIONS:
1. What does the term "rational consumers" mean in the context of the viewpoint?
2. What are "competitive" foods, and how do they factor into the authors' argument?
3. What conclusion did a 1994–1996 study of school lunches come to about the government's ability to fight obesity in schools?

O besity is one of the nation's most serious health problems. The news media are swamped by stories documenting that Americans of all ages are fatter than ever and that the long-term health consequences of the added weight are grave. In 1989, only 3 percent of the American public rated obesity as the most important U.S. health problem; by 2004 that figure had jumped to 16 percent. Only cancer (at 24 percent) ranked as a more important health problem than obesity.

Until recently, most Americans regarded weight as a matter of personal choice. But as the number of obese children has tripled over the past three decades, that laissez-faire [to let people do as they choose] view of obesity has grown to seem quaint, if not dangerous. . . . The serious health risks of obesity, combined with rapidly rising obesity-related health care costs, warrant not only public attention but also public action and spending.

A fifth grader picks up his lunch box prepared according to regulations in the Child Nutrition Act.

Why Public Intervention Is Needed

The first and most obvious reason for public action is that obesity is contributing substantially to the nation's exploding expenditures on health care. In 2002, the direct costs of treating obesity-related conditions such as diabetes, heart disease, renal failure, and hypertension were estimated at $92 billion to $117 billion. On top of that, indirect costs such as missed work and future earnings losses owing to premature death have been estimated at another $56 billion a year. Whether paid for primarily by tax dollars through Medicare or Medicaid or by private insurance, obesity-related health problems impose huge costs on the general public, not just the obese. Further, obese Americans suffer higher rates of disability and are sometimes forced to retire early, increasing the costs of the nation's financially strapped disability and retirement programs. Given the expected rapid growth of health and disability expenditures, containing these costs is vital to both the federal budget and the pocketbooks of all Americans. Reducing obesity is an important part of cost containment.

The Government Is Responsible for Children's Health

Government action is also called for because rates of obesity are rising especially fast among children. Under the law, children are judged incapable of making rational and fully informed choices. In terms used by economists, they are not "rational consumers." Moreover, a pervasive finding of research on child development is that actions taken in childhood have major impacts on adult status and behavior. Not only are obese children likely to grow up to be obese adults, but also eating and exercise habits established during childhood will importantly shape eating and exercise in adulthood. Moreover, as a recent report from the National Institute of Medicine shows, children's food preferences are strongly influenced by advertising—a policy area that offers ample precedent for government regulation. Although First Amendment issues lurk, the nation's several-decades-long experience with smoking demonstrates that a combination of government mandatory regulation and industry "voluntary" self-regulation can dramatically change the advertising climate for children and adults. Ronald McDonald, unless he changes his supersizing ways, should be headed toward [smoking icon] Joe Camel oblivion.

Taken together, these two arguments provide ample justification for government intervention to reduce childhood obesity. A host of policies and programs at the federal, state, and local level have been developed over the past decade or so to fight childhood obesity, and new programs and policies are certain to be developed in the years ahead. . . . These policies fall into four groups: prevention measures addressed to both children and parents; reduction of children's exposure to advertising of foods high in sugar and fat; improved delivery by pediatricians of preventive care and treatment for obesity and related medical conditions; and improved nutrition and physical activity within the schools. We believe that policies and programs implemented in the public schools hold the greatest promise.

Why Focus on Schools?

Children spend a large part of their lives in school. They begin attending school at age five—and in many cases, especially with children from low-income families, at age four or even three—and most remain there until age eighteen. Nearly every school in the nation serves at least one and often two meals a day, five days a week, over all these years. Schools have the opportunity, then, both to influence the nutrition children receive on a regular basis and to help children establish healthful lifelong eating habits. In addition, schools can help children get regular exercise and can offer courses on health maintenance, including proper diet and exercise. Because schools also have frequent contact with parents, they may be able to influence both the foods children consume at home and their parents' understanding of the importance of physical activity for their children's health. In short, schools offer a prime target for those like us who want to reduce rates of obesity and thereby promote child health.

Changing the Menu

Foods available in schools fall into three categories: the federal school lunch and breakfast programs, à la carte food items available in the school cafeteria, and foods available in vending machines and other venues outside the school cafeteria. Because the à la carte items and vending machines compete with school meals, they are often collectively referred to as competitive foods. Foods in these three categories, however, are subject to very different rules.

The federal lunch and breakfast programs are highly regulated by the U.S. Department of Agriculture (USDA). These meals are gradually becoming more nutritious, if not (by student report) exactly delicious.

By contrast, the à la carte items—thanks in part t(
nies that lobby Congress in Washington—are only
by the federal government. The items offered à la
from school to school, but foods high in fat and su
cookies are usually available. Some schools even al
dors such as Taco Bell, Subway, Domino's, and Piz
their products in the school cafeteria.

As part of its modest efforts to control consumption of unhealthful foods at school, the federal government has labeled certain foods,
including soda pop, water ices, chewing gum, and some candies, as
being of "minimal nutritional value" and has ruled that they cannot
be sold in the cafeteria during school meals. But many types of candy
and other unhealthful foods have escaped that label and are free to
compete directly with school meals in the cafeteria during lunch hour.
And schools can make even foods
of minimal nutritional value available outside the cafeteria during
lunch time and throughout the day
especially in vending machines.

Congress has on several occasions modified the school lunch
and breakfast programs, which
were reauthorized in 2004 as part
of an omnibus [comprehensive]
child nutrition law, to require
schools to make meals more attractive and nutritious. To some extent,
Congress, USDA, and local school authorities have worked together
to improve school meals. A study commissioned by USDA showed
that during the 1991–92 school year, lunches in nearly every school
served by the school lunch program failed to meet accepted guidelines for fat and saturated fats. In response, USDA promulgated new
standards to help school food service personnel reduce the fat content of meals and serve more nutritious food. A follow-up USDA
study, based on survey data for 1994–96, found that although most
schools still failed to meet the guidelines, the fat content of school
meals had declined substantially, proving that administrative action

> **FAST FACT**
>
> A 2009 study by the Centers for Disease Control and Prevention found that obesity-related health expenses may cost the United States as much as $147 billion each year.

federal government can directly affect the food consumed in
ation's schools. . . .

The Government Must Act

The public is now aware that obesity is a growing national problem,
and the news media nourish this awareness with a steady stream of
obesity-related stories. Recent actions by Congress, state legislatures,
and local school officials suggest a nascent commitment to fight child
obesity on several fronts—by restricting advertisements for unhealthful foods directed at children, by improving preventive care by pediatricians, and above all by ensuring that schools provide healthful and
appealing food and give children strenuous exercise on a daily basis.

> **EVALUATING THE AUTHORS'
> ARGUMENTS:**
>
> **Haskins, Paxson, and Donahue argue that American chil-
> dren need the government's help to fight obesity because
> they are not capable of making rational and informed de-
> cisions about food and health. Do you agree with this state-
> ment? Why or why not? Explain your reasoning and quote
> from the text in your answer.**

The Government Is Not Responsible for Helping People Lose Weight

Paul Hsieh

"*The Founders correctly understood that the proper role of government is to protect individual rights and otherwise leave men free to live—not tell us how many eggs we should eat.*"

The government has no right to help people lose weight argues Paul Hsieh in the following viewpoint. He warns Americans that inviting the government to solve the country's obesity problem will lead to the development of a "waistline police," which would infringe upon Americans' freedom by telling them what they can and cannot eat. He discusses examples from other countries in which people have been fined or denied immigration rights or access to government programs because they were deemed too overweight. Hsieh uses these examples to

Paul Hsieh, "Universal Healthcare and the Waistline Police: We Risk a Nanny State Contrary to American Ideals," *The Christian Science Monitor*, January 7, 2009. Reproduced by permission of the author.

argue against universal health care programs which make the government responsible for paying for citizens' health care costs. Hsieh says if the government is not responsible for the costs of obesity, it will not burden itself with taking control of Americans' personal choices. He concludes that individuals alone are responsible for their health—if they choose to be unhealthy it should be their right to do so.

Hsieh practices medicine in Colorado and is a cofounder of Freedom and Individual Rights in Medicine (FIRM), a group that promotes individual rights, personal responsibility, and free market economics in health care.

AS YOU READ, CONSIDER THE FOLLOWING QUESTIONS:
1. What advertisements does Hsieh say were banned by the British government? Upon whose right did this infringe?
2. What measures does Hsieh say certain American cities have taken to control their residents' weight and health? List at least two of them.
3. What would America's Founding Fathers be appalled to know, according to Hsieh?

I magine a country where the government regularly checks the waistlines of citizens over age 40. Anyone deemed too fat would be required to undergo diet counseling. Those who fail to lose sufficient weight could face further "reeducation" and their communities subject to stiff fines.

Is this some nightmarish dystopia?

No, this is contemporary Japan.

A "Nanny State on Steroids"

The Japanese government argues that it must regulate citizens' lifestyles because it is paying their health costs. This highlights one of the greatly underappreciated dangers of "universal healthcare." Any government that attempts to guarantee healthcare must also control its costs. The inevitable next step will be to seek to control citizens' health and their behavior. Hence, Americans should beware that if we adopt univer-

sal healthcare, we also risk creating a "nanny state on steroids" antithetical [in opposition] to core American principles.

Other countries with universal healthcare are already restricting individual freedoms in the name of controlling health costs. For example, the British government has banned some television ads for eggs on the grounds that they were promoting an unhealthy lifestyle. This is a blatant infringement of egg sellers' rights to advertise their products.

In 2007, New Zealand banned Richie Trezise, a Welsh submarine cable specialist, from entering the country on the grounds that his obesity would "impose significant costs . . . on New Zealand's health or special education services." Richie later lost weight and was allowed to immigrate, but his wife had trouble slimming and was kept home. Germany has mounted an aggressive anti-obesity campaign in workplaces and schools to promote dieting and exercise. Citizens who fail to cooperate are branded as "antisocial" for costing the government billions of euros in medical expenses.

Some people object to government efforts to prevent obesity, arguing that it will create a government "waistline police."

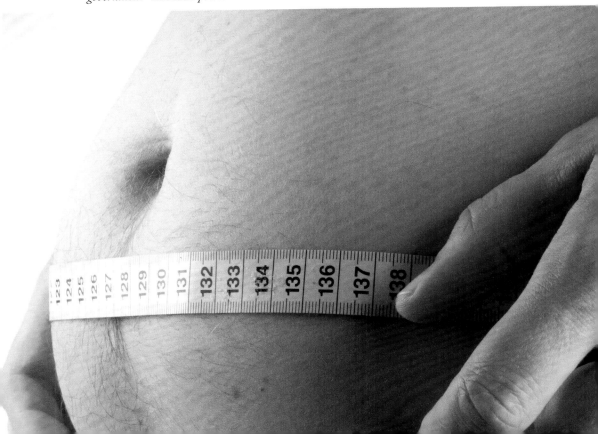

Health Is a Person's Responsibility— Not a Government's

Of course healthy diet and exercise are good. But these are issues of personal—not government—responsibility. So long as they don't harm others, adults should have the right to eat and drink what they wish— and the corresponding responsibility to enjoy (or suffer) the consequences of their choices. Anyone who makes poor lifestyle choices should pay the price himself or rely on voluntary charity, not demand that the government pay for his choices.

FAST FACT

A 2009 CBS News poll found that 89 percent of Americans view obesity as a problem that can be controlled with diet and exercise.

Government attempts to regulate individual lifestyles are based on the claim that they must limit medical costs that would otherwise be a burden on "society." But this issue can arise only in "universal healthcare" systems where taxpayers must pay for everyone's medical expenses.

Although American healthcare is only under partial government control in the form of programs such as Medicaid and Medicare, American nanny state regulations have exploded in recent years.

Many American cities ban restaurants from selling foods with trans fats. Los Angeles has imposed a moratorium on new fast food restaurants in South L.A. Other California cities ban smoking in some private residences. California has outlawed after-school bake sales as part of a "zero tolerance" ban on selling sugar products on campus. New York Gov. David Paterson has proposed an 18 percent tax on sugary sodas and juice drinks, and state officials have not ruled out additional taxes on cheeseburgers and other foods deemed unhealthy.

These ominous trends will only accelerate if the US adopts universal healthcare.

Americans Should Be Free to Eat and Drink What They Like

Just as universal healthcare will further fuel the nanny state, the nanny state mind-set helps fuel the drive toward universal healthcare. Individuals aren't regarded as competent to decide how to manage their lives and their health. So the government provides "cradle to grave" coverage of their healthcare.

Nanny state regulations and universal healthcare thus feed a vicious cycle of increasing government control over individuals. Both undermine individual responsibility and habituate citizens to ever-worsening erosions of their individual rights. Both promote dependence on government. Both undermine the virtues of independence and rationality. Both jeopardize the very foundations of a free society.

The American Founding Fathers who fought and died for our freedoms would be appalled to know their descendants were allowing the government to dictate what they could eat and drink. The Founders correctly understood that the proper role of government is to protect individual rights and otherwise leave men free to live—not tell us how many eggs we should eat.

(c) 2010 Bob Englehart, *The Hartford Courant*, and PoliticalCartoons.com.

If we still value our freedoms, we must reject both the nanny state and universal healthcare. Otherwise, it won't be long before the "Waistline Police" come knocking on our doors.

EVALUATING THE AUTHORS' ARGUMENTS:

Hsieh and the authors of the previous viewpoint disagree on whether the government bears any responsibility for safeguarding the personal health of its citizens. After reading both viewpoints, what is your opinion on this issue? Should the government institute programs that help its citizens be healthier? Or are such programs a violation of citizens' personal freedom to live as they choose? Explain your answer using evidence from the texts you have read.

The Government Should Tax Junk Food in Order to Curb Obesity

"The United States needs . . . a way to raise revenue for needed programs now and a way to lower healthcare costs in the future. Taxes on sugar-sweetened beverages . . . would answer that need."

Kelly D. Brownell and
David S. Ludwig

In the following viewpoint Kelly D. Brownell and David S. Ludwig propose that the state of California levy a small tax on soda in order to curb obesity. They say the benefits from such a program would be two-fold. First, proceeds from the tax could be used to fund badly needed public health care programs. Second, a tax might dissuade people from drinking soda in the first place, which would also improve their health. The authors argue that soda and other junk food should be taxed because they are outrageously bad for human health. They say it is wrong that soda companies have gotten rich by compromising the health of their customers, but a tax on their products could

Kelly D. Brownell and David S. Ludwig, "The Soda-Tax Solution," *Los Angeles Times*, October 6, 2009.
Copyright © 2009 *Los Angeles Times*. Reproduced by permission of the authors.

help right this injustice. For all of these reasons Brownell and Ludwig conclude that taxing soda and other junk food is an appropriate way to raise money that is badly needed to fight obesity.

Brownell is director of the Rudd Center for Food Policy and Obesity at Yale University. Ludwig is a professor of pediatrics at Harvard Medical School.

AS YOU READ, CONSIDER THE FOLLOWING QUESTIONS:
1. How much of a tax do the authors suggest be levied on each ounce of soda sold?
2. How much of the world beverage market do Brownell and Ludwig say is cornered by Coca-Cola and PepsiCo?
3. What percentage of California children do the authors say drink soda every day? How many calories does a regular twenty-ounce soda contain?

The United States needs a healthcare sweet spot—a way to raise revenue for needed programs now and a way to lower healthcare costs in the future. Taxes on sugar-sweetened beverages—those with added sugar, high-fructose corn syrup or so-called fruit juice concentrates—would answer that need, and California could be the test case that proves it once and for all.

A Small Tax Could Raise and Save Billions

There is arresting logic to the numbers. There are already minor surcharges on soda in many states—fractions of a cent per ounce in most cases. That's not enough. What's needed is a penny per ounce added to the cost of sugary beverages. That amount would raise about $150 billion nationally over the next 10 years; in California, it would raise $18 billion. At the same time, the reduced consumption of soft drinks produced by a penny-per-ounce national tax would have direct health benefits, estimated to be at least $50 billion over the decade. This $200 billion could make an enormous difference in addressing the nation's mounting healthcare costs.

The average American drinks 50 gallons of sugared beverages annually. Once dominated by a few flagship beverages such as Coke and

Two Reasons to Tax Soda

Both children and adults consume more sugar-sweetened beverages such as soda or energy drinks than milk or juice. Some argue that taxing these beverages can fight obesity in two ways: by raising money to fund public health programs and by encouraging people to buy fewer sugary drinks.

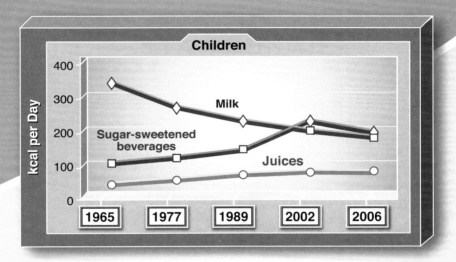

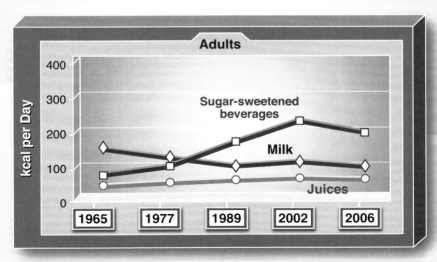

Taken from: Kelly D. Brownell et al., "The Public Health and Economic Benefit of Taxing Sugar-Sweetened Beverages," *New England Journal of Medicine*, October 15, 2009, p. 160.

Pepsi, the marketplace has exploded into a wide array of fruit drinks, sweetened teas, energy drinks, sports drinks and other versions of sugar water. But two companies still reign: Together, Coca-Cola and PepsiCo control three-quarters of the world beverage market.

Soda Has Hurt Americans' Health

Sugared beverages are marketed with fierce precision, using sports stars and other celebrities and promising benefits ranging from increased energy to better memory. Product placements in television shows, such as Coca-Cola on "American Idol," expose vast numbers of children to hidden marketing. Portions are also an issue—the 8-ounce bottle of the 1950s has morphed into a 20-ounce behemoth [something huge or enormous]. A regular 20-ounce soda contains 17 teaspoons of sugar and 250 calories.

The consequence? By the mid-1990s, per capita consumption of sugared beverages surpassed that of milk for children. Americans, including children, consume about 170 calories per day from these products, enough to have contributed substantially to the obesity epidemic and, independent of body weight, caused many cases of diabetes and heart disease. A recent study by UCLA and the California Center for Public Health Advocacy showed that 41% of California children drink soda every day, and that adults who drink soda are 27% more likely to be overweight or obese.

The industry has launched an all-out assault on "soda-pop taxes." Beverage companies and their front groups claim that it is unfair to pick on soda when there are many factors contributing to obesity.

However, the scientific evidence linking sugared beverages with weight gain is stronger than for any other food category. Also, sugar in liquid

> **FAST FACT**
>
> According to the office of New York governor David Paterson, an 18 percent tax on soda and other sugary drinks containing less than 70 percent fruit juice would raise $1 billion over two years and reduce the consumption of sugary drinks by 5 percent.

Soda drinks have been found to contribute to childhood obesity, and some state governments want to levy a tax on beverages to help pay for obesity-prevention programs.

form seems unique in its ability to slip past the body's calorie-detecting radar, perhaps because throughout evolution, the only beverage humans drank in large quantities beyond infancy was water. In other words, when you drink soda, you don't feel as full as if you were eating solid food, despite how many calories you're taking in. In addition, conventional sugared beverages lack fiber, antioxidants and other protective nutrients that might mitigate the adverse effects of their essentially empty calories on health.

Taxes Would Help Families in Need

The industry also claims that a beverage tax would hurt the poor (the same argument was used by tobacco companies to fight cigarette taxes). But as with tobacco, the poor are most hurt by diseases such as diabetes and obesity and stand to benefit the most from programs that could be supported by tax revenues. What's more, the average family could save several thousand dollars a year by cutting out soda. There is no question a tax would decrease consumption of sugar-sweetened beverages. Economists estimate a 10% price increase would result in a 10% consumption reduction. Otherwise, why would the beverage industry use a strategy from the tobacco playbook and establish a front group—Americans Against Food Taxes—meant to evoke images of a vast consumer uprising?

Congress has discussed a tax on sugared beverages as a means to fund healthcare but thus far has yielded to industry pressure and taken no action nationally. It is often the case, however, that states and cities take action before the federal government mobilizes. The California Legislature is set to hold hearings in November to consider taxes and fees on soda as a way of addressing obesity and healthcare problems in the state. With a penny-per-ounce decision, California could set an example for the rest of the country.

EVALUATING THE AUTHORS' ARGUMENTS:

To make their argument, Brownell and Ludwig discuss several ways in which a soda tax might help poor families. In one or two paragraphs, list each of these ways, then state whether you agree. In your opinion, are poor families who drink soda more likely to benefit or be harmed by taxes on soda? Why?

Junk Food Should Not Be Taxed

Colorado Springs Gazette

"It's an unfair control tax, and nothing more. View it not as a challenge to junk food, but as an affront to our freedom to choose."

In the following editorial published by the *Colorado Springs Gazette*, the author argues that junk food should not be taxed. It is unfair for the government to impose taxes on activities it decides it does not like, says the author. Although eating healthy food is important, for people to have the right to do what they like is more important—and this includes eating the foods they prefer without being forced to pay a premium for them. The government has no business making people who like junk food pay more for those foods just so the state can earn extra money. In the *Gazette*'s opinion, junk foods have been unfairly demonized—taxing them will not cause people to stop eating them or suddenly begin appreciating healthy foods. For this reason the author argues against taxing junk food on the grounds that it violates Americans' personal freedom and invites government control over their lives.

Gazette Editorial Staff, "A Junk Food Tax Erodes Freedom," *Gazette.com*, November 16, 2009. Copyright © 2009 Freedom Communications. Reproduced by permission.

AS YOU READ, CONSIDER THE FOLLOWING QUESTIONS:
1. Explain how the government uses taxes to discourage and encourage various activities, according to the author.
2. What, according to the author, is more important than good nutrition?
3. Why, according to the *Gazette*, should people who don't eat junk food still care about a tax imposed on such food?

I f we forget about the value of freedom and the joy of making choices for ourselves, it's easy to admire Gov. Bill Ritter's desire to eliminate a state sales tax exemption on candy and pop. After all, junk food rots teeth and makes some people fat and diabetic.

A primary tool of top-down social engineering is the imposition of taxes on activities government leaders would like to discourage. If government wants to discourage the burning of fossil fuels, it imposes higher taxes on oil and gas. This raises the price, and a price is nothing other than a control valve. In Economics 101 we learn that raising a price slows the consumption and trade of a product or service, while lowering a price increases consumption and trade.

Just as government is able to discourage activities with taxes, it has the option of encouraging activities with tax exemptions and rebates. The government wants couples to have kids, for example, and children come at great initial cost to their parents. To encourage reproduction, therefore, the government offers a substantial tax break for each child under a couple's care. To encourage philanthropy, the government offers exemptions to charities and churches and those who fund them. It's all social engineering, driven by government rather than a free market.

In Colorado, state government wants a slice of revenue from every financial transaction between buyer and seller. It achieves this with a sales tax. Government does not desire, however, to impede consumption of food. It does not want a tax on nutrition supplies even the poorest among us need in order to survive. Therefore, the state exempts taxes on most food products bought for consumption at home. The food exemption includes candy and pop, perhaps incidentally.

Ritter believes state government needs more money. He would also like to slow the consumption of candy and pop. Ritter, after all, formerly ran a nutrition center in Zambia, and he knows how excessive consumption of sugary treats may lead to tooth decay, obesity, and diabetes. By eliminating the tax exemption for unhealthy treats, the state would generate revenue and discourage consumption of processed sugar in one fell swoop.

At times like these, people who value freedom for freedom's sake must speak up for junk food junkies. Good nutrition is important; freedom is many times more important. That means one can live as a health-obsessed, organic-only vegan—on a crusade to improve youth nutrition—and oppose the governor's proposal for a junk food tax that makes it harder to choose candy and pop.

Those who don't consume junk food, and think they're immune from taxes imposed upon personal choices, should consider a controversy unfolding in Missouri. State officials, looking for any source of revenue they can find, have begun collecting sales taxes on yoga classes. Missouri officials consider yoga a form of recreation, while a growing number of yoga enthusiasts and instructors in Missouri have begun insisting yoga is religious—thus exempt from taxes.

> ## FAST FACT
>
> **A 2009 CBS News poll found that 72 percent of Americans think taxing junk food like soda, chips, and candy would not encourage people to lose weight.**

Fortunately, Colorado residents are wise enough to understand the ramifications of quick and easy changes to tax policies. In 1992 they amended the state constitution to forbid just the kind of social engineering Gov. Ritter wants to impose. The same law protects yoga, and all other activities, from new taxes.

The Colorado Constitution's Taxpayers Bill of Rights requires an election for: "a tax policy change directly causing a net tax revenue gain to any district." The law defines "district" as "the state or any local government, excluding enterprises." That's pretty clear. Eliminating an exemption is nothing other than a tax policy change resulting in a revenue gain.

Americans Do Not Favor Taxing Junk Food

The majority of Americans oppose levying a tax on junk food and do not think it would encourage people to lose weight.

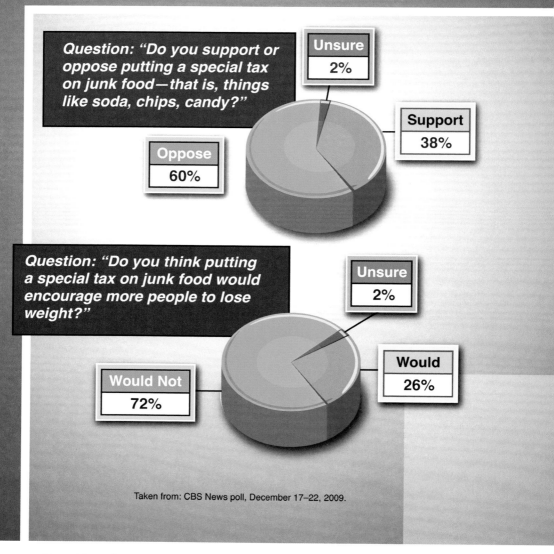

Question: "Do you support or oppose putting a special tax on junk food—that is, things like soda, chips, candy?"

Unsure
2%

Support
38%

Oppose
60%

Question: "Do you think putting a special tax on junk food would encourage more people to lose weight?"

Unsure
2%

Would
26%

Would Not
72%

Taken from: CBS News poll, December 17–22, 2009.

Gov. David Patterson, D-New York, walked away from an idea to impose taxes on soft drinks because opponents convinced him it would hit the poor hardest.

Gov. Ritter should follow Gov. Patterson's lead and abandon this idea. The tax would raise prices only for people who derive joy from choosing cheap junk food; it would do nothing to help them afford or appreciate Bok Choy from Whole Foods. It's an unfair control tax, and nothing more. View it not as a challenge to junk food, but as an affront to our freedom to choose.

EVALUATING THE AUTHORS' ARGUMENTS:

In this viewpoint the author characterizes a junk food tax as something that violates Americans' personal freedom and invites the government to control the lives and choices of its citizens. In the previous viewpoint the author characterizes a junk food tax as something that would help Americans feel better, stay healthier, save money, and have access to important public programs. After reading both viewpoints, with which author do you agree? If you could vote on the matter, would you support or oppose a junk food tax? Why or why not? Quote from both texts in your answer.

Overweight People Should Have to Pay More for Health Insurance

David Leonhardt

"The people imposing [a cost] on society should be required to pay it."

In the following viewpoint David Leonhardt suggests overweight Americans should have to pay more for health insurance. He explains that obesity is the foremost public health problem facing the country—expenses related to the treatment of obesity reach billions of dollars every year. Yet all Americans —whether fat or thin—are forced to pay for a portion of those bills, even if they have not benefited from the treatments. Leonhardt says this is not fair—people who rack up costs should primarily be the ones to pay them. Charging fat people more for health insurance, says Leonhardt, would have two main benefits: It would make overweight people personally responsible for a larger share of costs that are related to the treatment of their own health problems; and it would give them

David Leonhardt, "The Way We Live Now: Fat Tax," *The New York Times Magazine,* August 16, 2009. Copyright © 2009 by The New York Times Company. Reprinted with permission.

an incentive to lose weight. Leonhardt acknowledges that making over-weight Americans pay higher health insurance premiums is unlikely to be a popular idea, but he concludes this tough love approach to obesity could offer a real solution to America's obesity epidemic.

Leonhardt is a staff writer for the *New York Times Magazine*, where this viewpoint was originally published.

AS YOU READ, CONSIDER THE FOLLOWING QUESTIONS:

1. Who is Delos M. Cosgrove, and how does he factor into the author's argument?
2. What percentage of deaths does Leonhardt say is the result of substandard medical care? What percentage is due to a person's behavior?
3. In what ways does Leonhardt say the American environment has come to promote obesity? List at least three ways.

Two years ago [in 2007], the Cleveland Clinic stopped hiring smokers. It was one part of a "wellness initiative" that has won the renowned hospital—which President [Barack] Obama recently visited—some very nice publicity. The clinic has a farmers' market on its main campus and has offered smoking-cessation classes for the surrounding community. Refusing to hire smokers may be more hard-nosed than the other parts of the program. But given the social marginalization of smoking, the policy is hardly shocking. All in all, the wellness initiative seems to be a feel-good story.

A Tough Love Approach to Fatness

Which is why it is so striking to talk to Delos M. Cosgrove, the heart surgeon who is the clinic's chief executive, about the initiative. Cosgrove says that if it were up to him, if there weren't legal issues, he would not only stop hiring smokers. He would also stop hiring obese people. When he mentioned this to me during a recent phone conversation, I told him that I thought many people might consider it unfair. He was unapologetic.

"Why is it unfair?" he asked. "Has anyone ever shown the law of conservation of matter doesn't apply?" People's weight is a reflection

Obese Individuals Spend More on Health Care

Obese individuals spend more on both services and medication than daily smokers and heavy drinkers. For example, obese individuals spend approximately 36 percent more than the general baseline population on health services and 77 percent more on medications. Only aging has a greater effect—and only on expenditures for medications.

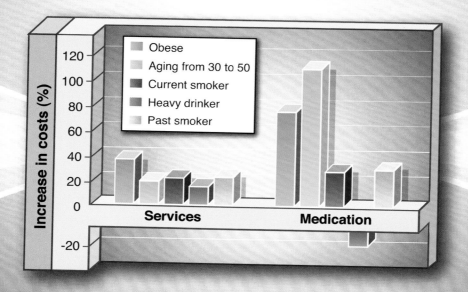

Baseline = comparable normal-weight individuals with no history of smoking or heavy drinking.

Taken from: "The Health Risks of Obesity: Worse than Smoking, Drinking, or Poverty," Rand Health, 2002, p. 2.

of how much they eat and how active they are. The country has grown fat because it's consuming more calories and burning fewer. Our national weight problem brings huge costs, both medical and economic. Yet our anti-obesity efforts have none of the urgency of our antismoking efforts. "We should declare obesity a disease and say we're going to help you get over it," Cosgrove said.

People Must Take Part in Improving Their Own Health

You can disagree with the doctor—you can even be offended—and still come to see that there is a larger point behind his tough-love approach. The debate over health care reform has so far revolved around how insurers, drug companies, doctors, nurses and government technocrats might be persuaded to change their behavior. And for the sake of the economy and the federal budget, they do need to change their behavior. But there has been far less discussion about how the rest of us might also change our behavior. It's as if we have little responsibility for our own health. We instead outsource it to something called the health care system.

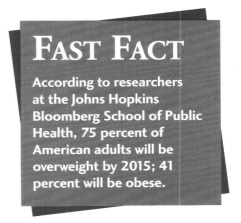

FAST FACT

According to researchers at the Johns Hopkins Bloomberg School of Public Health, 75 percent of American adults will be overweight by 2015; 41 percent will be obese.

The promise of that system is undeniably alluring: whatever your ailment, a pill or a procedure will fix it. Yet the promise hasn't been kept. For all the miracles that modern medicine really does perform, it is not the primary determinant of most people's health. J. Michael McGinnis, a senior scholar at the Institute of Medicine, has estimated that only 10 percent of early deaths are the result of substandard medical care. About 20 percent stem from social and physical environments, and 30 percent from genetics. The biggest contributor, at 40 percent, is behavior.

Charge Fat People More for Their Care

Today, the great American public-health problem is indeed obesity. The statistics have become rote, but consider that people in their 50s are about 20 pounds heavier on average than 50-somethings were in the late 1970s. As a convenient point of reference, a typical car tire weighs 20 pounds.

This extra weight has caused a sharp increase in chronic diseases, like diabetes, that are unusually costly. Other public-health scourges, like lung cancer, have tended to kill their victims quickly, which (in the most tragic possible way) holds down their long-term cost. Obesity is different. A recent article in *Health Affairs* estimated its annual cost to be $147 billion and growing. That translates into $1,250 per household, mostly in taxes and insurance premiums.

A natural response to this cost would be to say that the people imposing it on society should be required to pay it. Cosgrove mentioned to me an idea that some economists favor: charging higher health-insurance premiums to anyone with a certain body-mass index. Harsh? Yes. Fair? You can see the argument. And yet it turns out that the obese already do pay something resembling their fair share of medical costs,

Whether obese people should pay more for their health insurance is a matter of debate.

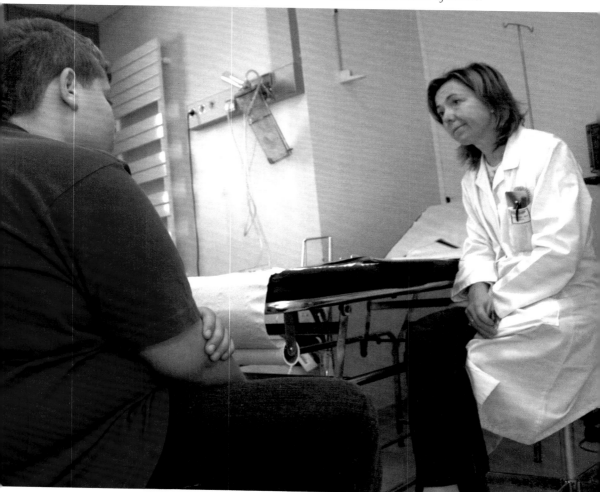

albeit in an indirect way. Overweight workers are paid less than similarly qualified, thinner colleagues, according to research by Jay Bhattacharya and M. Kate Bundorf of Stanford. The cause isn't entirely clear. But the size of the wage difference is roughly similar to the size of the difference in their medical costs.

It's also worth noting that the obese, as well as any of the rest of us suffering from a medical condition affected by behavior, already have plenty of incentive to get healthy. But we struggle to do so. Daily life gets in the way. Inertia triumphs.

The Question of Responsibility

The question of personal responsibility, then, ends up being more complicated than it may seem. It's hard to argue that Americans have collectively become more irresponsible over the last 30 years; the murder rate has plummeted, and divorce and abortion rates have fallen. And our genes certainly haven't changed in 30 years.

What has changed is our environment. Parents are working longer, and takeout meals have become a default dinner. Gym classes have been cut. The real price of soda has fallen 33 percent over the last three decades. The real price of fruit and vegetables has risen more than 40 percent.

The solutions to these problems are beyond the control of any individual. They involve a different sort of responsibility: civic—even political—responsibility. They depend on the kind of collective action that helped cut smoking rates nearly in half. Anyone who smoked in an elementary-school hallway today would be thrown out of the building. But if you served an obesity-inducing, federally financed meal to a kindergartner, you would fit right in. Taxes on tobacco, meanwhile, have skyrocketed. A modest tax on sodas—one of the few proposals in the various health-reform bills aimed at health, rather than health care—has struggled to get through Congress.

No Other Way to Cure an Epidemic

Cosgrove's would-be approach may have its problems. The obvious one is its severity. The more important one is probably its narrowness: not even one of the nation's most prestigious hospitals can do much to reduce obesity. The government, however, can. And that is the great virtue of Cosgrove's idea. He is acknowledging that any effort to attack obesity will inevitably involve making value judgments and even limiting people's choices. Most of the time, the government has no business doing such things. But there is really no other way to cure an epidemic.

EVALUATING THE AUTHORS' ARGUMENTS:

Leonhardt claims that fat Americans should pay more for health insurance because overweight people get sick more often and thus cost the system more. How would Daniel Engber, the author of the following viewpoint, respond to this claim? Write one paragraph that summarizes each author's position, and then state with which author you agree.

Viewpoint
6

Overweight Americans Should Not Have to Pay More for Health Insurance

Daniel Engber

"Insurance plans that discriminate according to body size are idiotic, unfair, and possibly illegal."

In the following viewpoint Daniel Engber argues that to charge overweight Americans more for health insurance is ineffective, discriminatory, and possibly illegal. He contends that not all fat people get sick at the same rate—some, in fact, are healthier than thin people. It would therefore be unfair to make them pay more just because they have a high body mass index (BMI). Engber says BMI is a bad way to identify overweight people in the first place. Some athletic or very muscular people tend to have a high BMI, but it would not make sense to charge them more for health insurance since they

Daniel Engber, "The Fat Premium: Congress Toys with a Silly Plan to Make Americans Lose Weight," *Slate.com*, October 29, 2009. Copyright © 2009 Washingtonpost.Newsweek Interactive. All Rights Reserved. Reproduced by permission.

are probably healthy. For others, the loss of just a few pounds is enough to change their BMI, which Engber says is not enough to significantly change their risk of disease. Finally, Engber says charging fat people more for health insurance would unfairly penalize the poor, since they are the ones least likely to be able to afford higher quality food or expensive weight loss equipment. For all of these reasons Engber concludes that charging fat people more for health insurance is an inappropriate—and possibly illegal—solution to the obesity crisis.

Engber is a senior editor at *Slate.com*, where this viewpoint was originally published.

AS YOU READ, CONSIDER THE FOLLOWING QUESTIONS:

1. What did a 2008 study from the *Archives of Internal Medicine* find about health and obesity? What bearing does this have on Engber's argument?
2. What law does Engber say might be violated if fat people are charged more for health insurance?
3. In what way might charging fat people more for health insurance constitute a violation of civil rights, according to Engber?

S afeway CEO Steven A. Burd thinks he's solved the nation's health care crisis. The California-based grocery chain has kept its insurance costs stable for the last four years, he says, while its competitors have watched their bills rise by an average of 38 percent. That's because Safeway encourages its workers to pursue a healthy lifestyle: If you're thin and you don't smoke, you can get a significant discount on your premiums. Otherwise, you've got two choices: Pay more for your insurance or mend your wicked ways.

Burd has spent the last several months making supersized claims about this incentive-based approach to health care. In June [2009], he told the Senate that if the government had adopted a Safeway-style program in 2004, we'd have saved $600 billion by now. That makes a federal soda tax look like peanuts.

It would be nice if these flashy numbers were verified by someone not wearing a Safeway management shirt. (The CEO variously describes them as coming from "my calculations" and "our calculations.")

Nevertheless, lawmakers from both parties, as well as President [Barack] Obama, are getting onboard with a Burd-inspired plan to help employer-sponsored insurance plans penalize fat people and smokers with higher premiums. The "Safeway Amendment," which was added to the Senate's health care bill earlier this month [October 2009] and has been proposed in the House, may soon end up as federal law.

There's only one problem: Insurance plans that discriminate according to body size are idiotic, unfair, and possibly illegal.

The History of Wellness Programs

I'll explain why in a minute, but let's start with a short lesson on how these Safeway-style "wellness programs" came to be. Back in 1996, Congress passed the Health Insurance Portability and Accountability Act [HIPAA], which forbade discrimination among members of group health plans according to their health status. That meant CEOs like Burd couldn't deny coverage or apply higher premiums to people who happened to be sickly or accident-prone; there could be no higher rates

Safeway CEO and president Steve Burd, right, participates in a roundtable discussion on health care reform before the U.S. Senate and discusses the advantages of Safeway's wellness programs.

for those who had congenital heart defects, or enjoyed skydiving, or happened to be morbidly obese. But the law left open the question of whether insurance plans could lower costs by encouraging healthy lifestyles through more exercise and better diets. In 2006, the federal government got around to clarifying the rules on "wellness programs." In the first place, there would be no limits on rewarding good behavior so long as everyone had equal access to the program. An insurance plan might reimburse members for joining a gym, for example, or entering a program to quit smoking. If participation were the only criterion for getting the reward, everything was legit.

The 2006 clarification also created a second, fuzzier category of wellness programs, in which a plan member's health status could indeed be used against him. Under certain conditions, the government said, a company could set up a system of payouts contingent on an employee's achieving specific health goals. The plan might lower your premium if you joined a gym and *lost weight*, or entered a program to quit smoking and *actually succeeded*. That's the kind of program Steven Burd has in place at Safeway: Instead of paying workers to exercise, Safeway pays them to lose weight or stay thin. (In terms of insurance premiums, that's the same as charging them extra money for being fat.) . . .

Not All Fat People Have Higher Health Care Costs

OK, what's so bad about penalizing workers for being fat?

The most egregious flaw in the Safeway program is the way it treats body size as a risk factor in and of itself. Yes, obesity is correlated with higher rates of cardiovascular disease, diabetes, and other ailments—but that doesn't mean that everyone who's fat is going to get sick. A 2008 study from the *Archives of Internal Medicine* found that a full one-third of all obese patients were "metabolically healthy" in terms of their blood pressure, cholesterol levels, and other measures. Meanwhile, one-fourth of the patients whose BMI was in the normal range showed *abnormal* metabolic signs. So a policy that varies its premiums as a function of body size is guaranteed to punish a bunch of people who are perfectly healthy and reward a bunch of people who are at risk. (According to the study, these backward incentives would affect about 18 percent of the population.)

Body Mass Index Is a Poor Measure of Health

Safeway's body-size threshold also ensures that some discounts would be doled out on the basis of trivial differences in body composition. If someone with a BMI of 30.1 trims down to 29.8, has he really reduced his risk of disease? (For someone who's 6 feet tall, that means losing two pounds.) The body mass index was never meant to be used for diagnosing individuals: It's a notoriously sloppy measure that can't distinguish between lean and fatty tissue. Those with athletic builds are often misclassified as being overweight or obese, and some researchers have found that exercise actually leads people to put on weight. Perversely, the Safeway plan could incentivize some of its members to *stop exercising*. Indeed, by making premium discounts contingent on weight loss rather than healthy behavior, Burd's program may encourage fat people to trim down at any cost. A sensible diet with lots of fruits and vegetables may be less effective than voluntary starvation—or even gastric bypass surgery, which carries its own grave risks and side effects.

> ## FAST FACT
>
> A study by the U.S. Department of Agriculture's Economic Research Service found that white women who are sixty-four or more pounds overweight tend to earn 9 percent less than their fit counterparts. This is equivalent to the difference in salary associated with 1.5 years of education or 3 years of work experience.

The fact that significant weight loss is nearly impossible to maintain poses yet another problem for outcome-based wellness plans. It's a safe bet that any obese person who manages to score the Safeway discount in a given year will be back in the penalty a few years later. That means plan members are incentivized to enter a cycle of yo-yo dieting, which may actually increase their risks of cardiovascular disease (although not all researchers agree on the dangers of weight cycling).

Penalizing the Poor

Even if the Safeway incentives did encourage healthy behavior, their implementation would almost certainly be unfair. Much of the criticism of Burd's amendment—and there's been plenty—has focused on the ways in which the program might single out people who are already impoverished. As I've said before, being poor can make you fat, and being fat can make you poor. Rates of obesity and poverty are closely linked across the country, and—among women, at least—the more money you have, the thinner you'll be.

In other words, the workers most likely to run afoul of Safeway's BMI threshold are those most burdened by the process of losing weight. Members of the skinny elite can treat themselves to pricey gym memberships, luxe organic produce, or a piece of the $60 billion diet industry. What about the folks who can't afford to pay for Gyrotonic? Sorry, higher premiums. If you're fat because you're poor, the Safeway penalty makes you poorer still—and that in turn makes it harder to lose weight. This Catch-22 [a no-win situation] may end up pricing the neediest members out of the system—and it could explain Burd's alleged success at cutting health care costs.

A Discriminatory Idea

On top of all of this, Safeway-style wellness programs must be carefully designed to accommodate federal and state laws. Last year [in 2008], a pair of public health experts from Harvard, Michelle Mello and Meredith Rosenthal, reviewed the legal limits of lifestyle discrimination in a paper for the *New England Journal of Medicine*. They considered all the ways that a program might be against the law, even if it meets the criteria set out in the HIPAA regulations. Charging fat people higher premiums might violate the Americans With Disabilities Act, for example, which protects the health benefits of anyone with an "impairment" caused by a "physiological condition." (So far, there's no clear precedent on whether obesity qualifies as such.) A Safeway-style program could also be challenged on civil rights grounds: Obesity rates are higher among blacks than whites, yet blacks tend to have less visceral fat given the same BMI. And then there's the fact that most states in the union prohibit employment discrimination on the basis of certain behaviors—like smoking—that are conducted outside of working hours. (Michigan specifically bans weight-based discrimination.) Given these concerns, and several others, Mello and Rosenthal concluded their analysis with "an overarching litmus test of program legality: health plan sponsors of wellness programs cannot 'pay for performance'—they can pay only for participation."

Nothing about the Safeway Amendment makes sense. When the Senate finance committee approved its version of the health reform package earlier this month, Chairman Max Baucus announced that his bill would extend coverage to almost every American, and that it "would prohibit insurance companies from discriminating on the basis of gender or health status." If Congress really wants equal access to medical care, why are we fattening a loophole for discrimination?

EVALUATING THE AUTHOR'S ARGUMENTS:

In this viewpoint Engber accuses people who suggest making overweight people pay more for health insurance of discriminating against not just overweight people but against poor people too. What pieces of evidence did he provide to support this claim? Did he convince you of his argument? Explain why or why not.

Editor's note: These facts can be used in reports to add credibility when making important points or claims.

Obesity Around the World

According to the World Health Organization:

- Worldwide, more than 1 billion adults are overweight.
- At least 300 million of them are obese.
- Obesity and overweight pose a major risk for chronic diseases, including type 2 diabetes, cardiovascular disease, hypertension and stroke, and certain forms of cancer.
- The key causes of obesity are increased consumption of energy-dense foods high in saturated fats and sugars and reduced physical activity.
- An estimated 22 million children under the age of five are estimated to be overweight worldwide.
- Obesity accounts for 2 to 7 percent of total health care costs in several developed countries.

The following ten nations have the highest percentages of adults who are obese (have BMIs of 30 or greater):

1. Nauru (78.53 percent)
2. American Samoa (74.6 percent)
3. Tokelau (63.4 percent)
4. Tonga (56 percent)
5. Kiribati (50.6 percent)
6. French Polynesia (40.9 percent)
7. Saudi Arabia (35.6 percent)
8. Panama (34.74 percent)
9. United States (33.9 percent)
10. United Arab Emirates (33.74 percent)

The following ten nations have the highest percentages of adults who are overweight (have BMIs of between 25 and 29.9):

1. American Samoa (93.5 percent)
2. Kiribati (81.5 percent)

3. French Polynesia (73.68 percent)
4. Saudi Arabia (72.5 percent)
5. Panama (67.43 percent)
6. United States (66.7 percent)
7. Germany (66.5 percent)
8. Egypt (66 percent)
9. Kuwait (64.16 percent)
10. Bosnia and Herzegovina (62.9 percent)

The following ten nations have the highest percentages of adults who have normal weights (have BMIs of between 18.5 and24.99):

1. Thailand (87.4 percent)
2. Lao People's Democratic Republic (77.1 percent)
3. Ghana (72.4 percent)
4. Philippines (69.51 percent)
5. Madagascar (69.08 percent)
6. Japan (68.9 percent)
7. Viet Nam (68.5 percent)
8. Mongolia (66.6 percent)
9. South Korea (63.2 percent)
10. India (62.5 percent)

Obesity in the United States

According to the National Center for Health Statistics:

- Sixty-seven percent of adults are overweight or obese,
- 34 percent of adults are obese,
- 18 percent of adolescents ages 12–19 years are overweight,
- 15 percent of children ages 6–11 years are overweight, and
- 11 percent of children ages 2–5 years are overweight.
- Black Americans have a 51 percent higher prevalence of obesity compared with whites.
- Hispanics have a 21 percent higher prevalence of obesity compared with whites.
- Just one state—Colorado—has a prevalence of obesity less than 20 percent.
- Thirty-two states have a prevalence equal to or greater than 25 percent.
- Six of these states—Alabama, Mississippi, Oklahoma, South Carolina, Tennessee, and West Virginia—have a prevalence of obesity equal to or greater than 30 percent.

According to the American Obesity Association:
- Approximately 127 million adults in the United States are overweight, 60 million are obese, and 9 million are severely obese.
- In 1980, 46 percent of the population was overweight; in 2000, 64.5 percent of the population was overweight.
- In 1980, 14.4 percent of the population was obese; in 2000, 30.5 percent of the population was obese.
- In 1994, 2.9 percent of the population was severely obese; in 2000, 4.7 percent of the population was severely obese.
- Obesity increases the risk of illness from about thirty serious medical conditions.
- Obesity is associated with increases in deaths from all causes.
- Earlier onset of obesity-related diseases, such as type 2 diabetes, are being reported in children and adolescents with obesity.
- Individuals with obesity are at higher risk for impaired mobility.
- Overweight or obese individuals experience social stigmatization and discrimination in employment and academic situations.
- The prevalence of overweight is higher for men (67 percent) than women (62 percent).
- The prevalence of obesity is higher for women (34 percent) than men (27.7 percent) as is severe obesity; women (6.3 percent) and men (3.1 percent).
- Obesity prevalence has increased across all education levels but is higher for persons with less education.

American Opinions About Obesity

According to a 2009 CBS News poll:
- Two percent of Americans would give the U.S. an "A" for its efforts to combat obesity;
- 18 percent of Americans would give the U.S. a "B" for its efforts to combat obesity;
- 35 percent of Americans would give the U.S. a "C" for its efforts to combat obesity;
- 27 percent of Americans would give the U.S. a "D" for its efforts to combat obesity;
- 14 percent of Americans would give the U.S. an "F" for its efforts to combat obesity;
- 89 percent of Americans view obesity as a problem that can be controlled with diet and exercise;

- 7 percent think it cannot be controlled with diet and exercise;
- 4 percent are unsure.

When asked to describe the seriousness of the problem of obesity:

- Fifty-seven percent of Americans describe obesity as a very serious public health problem;
  - 47 percent of men describe obesity as a very serious public health problem,
  - 66 percent of women describe obesity as a very serious public health problem.
- Thirty-eight percent of Americans describe obesity as a somewhat serious public health problem;
  - 44 percent of men describe obesity as a somewhat serious public health problem,
  - 32 percent of women describe obesity as a somewhat serious public health problem.
- Four percent of Americans say obesity is not a very serious public health problem;
  - 7 percent of men say obesity is not a very serious public health problem,
  - 1 percent of women say obesity is not a very serious public health problem.
- One percent of Americans say obesity is not a serious problem at all;
  - 1 percent of men say obesity is not a serious problem at all,
  - 0 percent of women say obesity is not a serious problem at all.

When asked if they would like to lose weight:

- Fifty-five percent of Americans said they would like to lose weight;
  - 47 percent of American men said they would like to lose weight,
  - 62 percent of American women said they would like to lose weight.
- Forty percent of Americans said they would like to stay at their present weight;
  - 45 percent of American men said they would like to stay at their present weight,
  - 43 percent of American women said they would like to stay at their present weight.
- Five percent of Americans said they would like to put on weight;
  - 8 percent of American men said they would like to put on weight,
  - 2 percent of American women said they would like to put on weight.

Organizations to Contact

The editors have compiled the following list of organizations concerned with the issues debated in this book. The descriptions are derived from materials provided by the organizations. All have publications or information available for interested readers. The list was compiled on the date of publication of the present volume; the information provided here may change. Be aware that many organizations take several weeks or longer to respond to inquiries, so allow as much time as possible for the receipt of requested materials.

Center for Science in the Public Interest (CSPI)
1875 Connecticut Ave. NW, Ste. 300
Washington, DC 20009
(202) 332-9110
Web site: www.cspinet.org

CSPI considers itself to be the organized voice of the American public on nutrition, food safety, health, and other issues. CSPI seeks to educate the public, advocate government policies that are consistent with scientific evidence on health and environmental issues, and counter industry's powerful influence on public opinion and public policies. CSPI supports food labeling campaigns and government efforts aimed at reducing the amount of sugar, salt, and fat Americans eat.

Centers for Disease Control and Prevention (CDC) Division of Nutrition and Physical Activity (DNPA)
1600 Clifton Rd.
Atlanta, GA 30333
(800) 232-4636
e-mail: cdcinfo@cdc.gov
Web site: www.cdc.gov

The CDC is part of the National Institutes of Health (NIH), Department of Health and Human Services. Its Division of Nutrition and Physical Activity has three focus areas: nutrition, physical activity, and overweight and obesity. The DNPA addresses the role of nutrition and physical activity in improving the public's health. DNPA activities include health promotion, research, training, and education. The DNPA maintains an overweight and obesity Web page which provides research-based information for consumers.

Coalition for Responsible Nutrition Information
(866) 764-0701
e-mail: info@nationalnutritionstandards.com
Web site: www.nationalnutritionstandards.com

This group seeks to provide consumers with comprehensive nutrition information about the food they consume while dining out so they are able to make healthy and informed decisions about their nutrition. Its Web site offers information about legislation regarding food labeling and recent news articles on the topic.

Food Research and Action Center (FRAC)
1875 Connecticut Ave. NW, Ste. 540
Washington, DC 20009
(202) 986-2200
Web site: www.frac.org

The Food Research and Action Center is the leading national nonprofit organization working to improve public policies and public-private partnerships to eradicate hunger and undernutrition in the United States. FRAC has published several papers about the link between hunger and obesity and works with hundreds of national, state, and local nonprofit organizations, public agencies, and corporations to address this and other food-related problems plaguing Americans.

International Association for the Study of Obesity (IASO)
28 Portland Pl.
London W1B 1LY
United Kingdom
+44 (0) 207 467 9610
Web site: www.iotf.org

The IASO is a nongovernmental organization with forty-nine member associations representing fifty-three countries. The mission of the IASO is to improve global health by promoting the understanding of obesity and weight-related diseases through scientific research and discussion. The IASO works with the World Health Organization (WHO) and other global nongovernmental organizations toward this goal.

Obesity Action Coalition (OAC)
4511 N. Himes Ave., Ste. 250
Tampa, FL 33614
(800) 717-3117
e-mail: info@obesityaction.org
Web site: www.obesityaction.org

The OAC is a not-for-profit organization that educates not only obesity patients but also their family members and the public. It provides links to resources and obesity support groups throughout the United States. The OAC works against the negative stigma of obesity and is an advocate for safe and effective obesity treatment.

The Obesity Awareness & Solutions Trust (TOAST)
The Latton Bush Centre
Southern Way
Harlow, Essex, UK CM18 7BL
+44 (0) 1279 866010
e-mail: enquiries@toast-uk.org.uk
Web site: www.toast-uk.org.uk

This British organization promotes the idea that obesity is a complex problem with no single solution. It says that the treatment and prevention of obesity must go beyond the medical model of diet, exercise, and medication.

The Obesity Society
8630 Fenton St., Ste. 814
Silver Spring, MD 20910
(301) 563-6526
Web site: www.obesity.org

The Obesity Society is the leading scientific society dedicated to the study of obesity. Since 1982, the society has been committed to encouraging research on the causes and treatment of obesity and to keeping the medical community and public informed of new advances.

Overeaters Anonymous (OA)
PO Box 44020
Rio Rancho, NM 87174-4020
(505) 891-2664
e-mail: info@oa.org
Web site: www.oa.org

Overeaters Anonymous is an organization open to individuals who wish to be, or who are, recovering from compulsive overeating. Individuals share their experiences and support each other to stop eating compulsively. OA provides a twelve-step program, modeled after the twelve-step program of Alcoholics Anonymous, to help members control their food addictions. Members can attend face-to-face meetings in their own localities and can communicate with members worldwide via the Internet.

Rudd Center for Food Policy & Obesity
Yale University
PO Box 208369
New Haven, CT 06520-8369
Web site: www.yaleruddcenter.org

This is a nonprofit research and public policy organization devoted to improving the world's diet, preventing obesity, and reducing weight stigma. The center serves as a leading research institution and clearinghouse for resources that add to the understanding of the complex forces affecting how we eat, how we stigmatize overweight and obese people, and how we can change.

Weight-Control Information Network (WIN)
1 WIN Way
Bethesda, MD 20892-3665
e-mail: win@info.niddk.nih.gov
Web site: http://win.niddk.nih.gov

WIN is an information service of the National Institute of Diabetes and Digestive and Kidney Diseases. It provides science-based and up-to-date information on weight control, obesity, physical activity, and related nutritional issues.

For Further Reading

Books

Albritton, Robert. *Let Them Eat Junk: How Capitalism Creates Hunger and Obesity.* London: Pluto, 2009. Analyzes the food industry from a Marxist perspective by detailing the economic relations that have put Americans in a situation of simultaneous oversupply and undersupply of food.

Finkelstein, Eric A., and Laurie Zuckerman. *The Fattening of America: How the Economy Makes Us Fat, If It Matters, and What to Do About It.* Wiley, 2008. Argues that modern technology makes producing higher-calorie processed goods cheap, which decreases our activity level and puts our health in danger. Debunks myths about the long-range cost of food production and consumption and argues America's obesity problem is costing it too much money and even hurting it militarily.

Kessler, David. *The End of Overeating: Taking Control of the Insatiable American Appetite.* Red Oak, IA: Rodale, 2009. Surveys the world of modern industrial food production and distribution and finds that Americans are systematically overexposed to foods loaded with sugar, salt, and fat.

Meana, Marta, and Lindsey Ricciardi. *Obesity Surgery: Stories of Altered Lives.* Reno: University of Nevada Press, 2008. The surprising and unpredictable story of the personal and social after-effects of rapid and dramatic weight loss. Using in-depth, first person accounts of thirty-three men and women, this book elaborates on the complexities of weight-loss surgery.

Oliver, J. Eric. *Fat Politics: The Real Story Behind America's Obesity Epidemic.* New York: Oxford University Press, 2005. Argues that America's obesity epidemic is largely the creation of doctors, politicians, and health officials who have ties to the diet and drug industry.

Power, Michael L., and Jay Schulkin. *The Evolution of Obesity.* Baltimore: Johns Hopkins University Press, 2009. Attempts to explain people's expanding waistlines by reviewing various studies of human and animal fat use and storage. Studies include those that examine fat deposition and metabolism in men and women; chronicle cultural differences in food procurement, preparation, and consumption; and consider the influence of sedentary occupations and lifestyles. Also discusses the consequences of being overweight for different demographic groups.

Smith, Patricia K. *Obesity Among Poor Americans: Is Public Assistance the Problem?* Nashville, TN: Vanderbilt University Press, 2009. Examines the controversial claim put forth by welfare critics that public assistance programs like Food Stamps and the National School Lunch programs contribute to obesity among the poor.

Stroebe, Wolfgang. *Dieting, Overweight, and Obesity: Self-Regulation in a Food-Rich Environment.* Washington, DC: American Psychological Association, 2008. Examines why self-regulation of weight is so difficult for many people. The author explains the history of body-weight standards, details the emotional and physical consequences of being overweight, and explores the various treatment and prevention plans for obesity.

Periodicals and Internet Sources

Allen, Marshall. "The Hidden Cost of Obesity," *Las Vegas Sun*, July 12, 2009. www.lasvegassun.com/news/2009/jul/12/hidden-cost-obesity.

Ambinder, Mark. "Fat Nation: It's Worse Than You Think," *Atlantic*, May 2010.

Armour, Nancy. "PE Requirement Isn't Enough to Fight Obesity," Physorg.com, June 16, 2009. www.physorg.com/news164339754.html.

Basham, Patrick, and John Luik. "Is the Obesity Epidemic Exaggerated? Yes," *British Medical Journal*, February 2, 2008. www.cato.org/pubs/articles/basham_obesity.html.

Berman, Richard. "Americans Should Still Have a Right to Guilt-Free Eating," *Palm Springs (CA) Desert Sun*, October 2, 2007. www.consumerfreedom.com/oped_detail.cfm/o/477-americans-should-still-have-a-right-to-guilt-free-eating.

Bialik, Carl. "The Slimming Figures of Childhood Obesity," *Wall Street Journal*, July 22, 2009. http://online.wsj.com/article/SB124821547930269995.html.

Brill, Alex, and Aparna Mathur. "A Fat Tax That's Hard to Swallow," *American*, June 12, 2009. www.american.com/archive/2009/june/a-fat-tax-that2019s-hard-to-swallow.

Brownell, Kelly D., et al. "The Public Health and Economic Benefits of Taxing Sugar-Sweetened Beverages," *New England Journal of Medicine*, October 15, 2009. http://content.nejm.org/cgi/reprint/ 361/16/1599.pdf.

Downs, Julie S., George Lowenstein, and Jessica Wisdom. "Eating by the Numbers," *New York Times*, November 13, 2009. www.nytimes .com/2009/11/13/opinion/13lowenstein.html.

Dubois, Pierre. "Obesity's on the Rise—Let's Have the Courage to Tax Junk Food!" Centre for Economic Policy Research, October 17, 2007. www.voxeu.org/index.php?q=node/635.

Economist. "Waist Banned," July 30, 2009. www.economist.com/busi nessfinance/displaystory.cfm?story_id=14120903.

Engber, Daniel. "Glutton Intolerance: What If a War on Obesity Only Makes the Problem Worse?" *Slate.com*, October 5, 2009. www.slate .com/id/2231508.

————. "Let Them Drink Water! What a Fat Tax Really Means for America," *Slate.com*, September 21, 2009. www.slate.com/id/ 2228713/pagenum/all/#p2.

Engelhard, Carolyn L., Arthur Garson Jr., and Stan Dorn. "Reducing Obesity: Policy Strategies from the Tobacco Wars," Urban Institute, July 2009. www.urban.org/uploadedpdf/411926_reducing_obesity.pdf.

Herper, Matthew. "The Hidden Cost of Obesity," *Forbes*, November 24, 2006. www.forbes.com/2006/07/19/obesity-fat-costs-cx-mh-0720obesity.html.

Hicks, Marybeth. "Child Obesity in Nanny State," *Washington Times*, February 24, 2010. www.washingtontimes.com/news/2010/feb/24/ hicks-child-obesity-in-nanny-state.

Hobson, Katherine. "To Eat Healthier, Skip Restaurants and Head for the Kitchen," *U.S. News and World Report*, May 27, 2008. www.usnews.com/health/blogs/on-fitness/2008/5/27/to-eat-healthier-skip-restaurants-and-head-for-the-kitchen.html.

Kiley, David. "Fast Food Menu Calorie Counter Should Be National Law," *BusinessWeek*, July 17, 2009. www.businessweek.com/the_ thread/brandnewday/archives/2009/07/fast_food_menu.html.

McArdle, Megan, interview with Paul Campos. "America's Moral Panic over Obesity," *Atlantic*, July 29, 2009. http://meganmcardle.theatlantic .com/archives/2009/07/americas_moral_panic_over_obes.php.

McKay, Betsy. "Cost of Treating Obesity Soars," *Wall Street Journal*, July 28, 2009. http://online.wsj.com/article/SB10001424052 970204563304574314794089897258.html.

O'Hagen, Maureen. "New Calorie Information on Restaurant Menus Causes Barely a Hiccup," *Seattle Times*, January 3, 2009. http://seattletimes.nwsource.com/html/foodwine/2008585699_restaurants03m.html.

Ridley, John. "Forget a 'Fat Tax.' Tax the Fat," *Huffington Post*, September 11, 2009. www.huffingtonpost.com/john-ridley/forget-a-fat-tax-tax-the_b_283868.html.

Rigby, Neville. "Obesity: What a Waist," *Guardian*, November 9, 2009. www.guardian.co.uk/commentisfree/2009/nov/09/obesity-health.

Robert Wood Johnson Foundation. "Menu Labeling: Does Providing Nutrition Information at the Point of Purchase Affect Consumer Behavior?" June 2009. www.rwjf.org/files/research/20090630hermenulabeling.pdf.

Roberto, Christina A., et al. "Evaluating the Impact of Menu Labeling on Food Choices and Intake," *American Journal of Public Health*, December 17, 2009. www.yaleruddcenter.org/resources/upload/docs/what/policy/ImpactMenuLabeling AJPH_12.09.pdf.

Ruiz, Rudy. "A Fat Tax Is a Healthy Idea," CNN.com, October 5, 2009. www.cnn.com/2009/POLITICS/10/05/ruiz.obesity.tax/index.html.

Stier, Jeff. "F Is for Fat—a Bad Idea," *Huffington Post*, June 11, 2007. www.huffingtonpost.com/jeff-stier/f-is-for-fat-a-bad-ide_b_51693.html.

Sullum, Jacob. "Are You *Sure* You Want Fries with That? Mandatory Calorie Counts Cross the Line Between Informing and Nagging," *Reason*, August 20, 2008. www.reason.com/news/show/128178.html.

Whitefield, Trice. "Leave Calorie Counts Off the Menu; Nutrition Is More Complex Than a Few Figures Can Convey," *Los Angeles Times*, July 22, 2008. www.consumerfreedom.com/oped_detail.cfm/o/577-leave-calorie-counts-off-the-menu-nutrition-is-more-complex-than-a-few-figures-can-convey.

Zarembo, Alan. "Childhood Obesity Rate in U.S. Hits a Plateau," *Los Angeles Times*, May 28, 2008. http://articles.latimes.com/2008/may/28/science/sci-obesity28.

Zinczenko, David. "Feeding the Obesity Epidemic," *USA Today*, March 25, 2008. http://blogs.usatoday.com/oped/2008/03/feeding-the-obe.html.

Web Sites

Centers for Disease Control and Prevention Obesity Page (www.cdc.gov/obesity). This site, run by the CDC, contains national data and statistics about obesity and overweight, along with information about specific state obesity programs. An excellent resource for reports.

The Mayo Clinic's Calorie Calculator (www.mayoclinic.com/health/calorie-calculator/nu00598). This site, run by the Mayo Clinic, allows users to estimate the number of calories needed daily to maintain a person's current body weight.

National Institutes of Health Body Mass Index Calculator (www.nhlbisupport.com/bmi). Body mass index (BMI) is a measure of body fat based on height and weight. This government site allows users to calculate their BMI and assess whether they are underweight, normal, overweight, or obese.

Obesity in America (www.obesityinamerica.org). Run by the Endocrine Society and the Hormone Foundation, this site contains a plethora of information about obesity in America. The maps, fact sheets, and brief articles are excellent for students researching reports on the topic.

Obesity Myths (www.obesitymyths.com). Run by the Center for Consumer Freedom, this site's thoughtful articles and statistics debunk the conventional wisdom that obesity is an epidemic plaguing Americans.

***Washington Post*'s Fast Food Calorie Counter** (www.washingtonpost.com/wp-srv/flash/health/caloriecounter/caloriecounter.html). This *Washington Post* site offers a calorie menu of the dishes at the nation's most popular fast food restaurants.

Index

A

Adolescents
  obese, 41, 44
Adults
  obesity rates in, 13–14
  trends in soda consumption
    by, *101*
Advertising, 89
Ambinder, Marc, 8, 9
American Academy of Child
  and Adolescent Psychology, 44
American Enterprise Institute, 8
*American Journal of Preventive
  Medicine,* 28
*American Journal of Public
  Health,* 52
Apovian, Caroline, 59
Archives of Internal Medicine
  (journal), 120
Auerbach, John, 60

B

Baltimore Obesity Initiative, 79
Baltimore Sun (newspaper), 82
Basham, Patrick, 19
Baucus, Max, 123
Blair, Steven, 36
Body mass index (BMI), 79, 83
  defining obesity/overweight by,
    34–35
  is poor measure of health, 81,
    121

waist-to-hip ratio and, 35
Brownell, Kelly D., 37, 99
Bundorf, M. Kate, 115
Bundred, Steve, 47
Burd, Steve, *119,* 120
Burd, Steve A., 118

C

California Center for Public
  Health Advocacy, 66
Calories
  increase in daily intake of, 9,
    15
  reduction in, 53–54
  from soda consumption, 102
Campos, Paul, 33, 34, 35, 36,
  37
Cancer, 28
Caravan Opinion Research
  Corporation, 54
CBS News poll, 96, 107
Centers for Disease Control and
  Prevention (CDC), 32, 49, 91
Cheh, Mary M., 71, 73, 74
Children
  food choices of, 89
  government is responsible for
    health of, 89–90
  obesity is declining among,
    23
  obesity rates among, 44, 49,
    77

is a personal responsibility, 96
Health Affairs (journal), 60, 114
Health-care costs
  increase in, *112*
  obesity-related, 13, 64, 88–89,
    91
Health insurance
  overweight people should pay
    more, 110–116
  overweight people should not
    pay more, 117–123
Health Insurance Portability
  and Accountability Act
  (HIPAA), 119
Health Survey for England, 21
Healthy Schools Act
  (Washington, D.C.), 71, 73
Hicks, Marybeth, 7
Hsieh, Paul, 93
Huckabee, Mike, 79

I
Illness(es)
  chronic, *29*
  obesity-associated, 25–30
Insurance. *See* Health insurance

J
Jacoby, Jeff, 57
Johns Hopkins Bloomberg
  School of Public Health, 113
*Journal of the American Medical
  Association*, 20, 33
Junk food
  does not cause obesity, 23
  government should not tax,
    105–109

government should tax,
  99–104
Junk food tax
  benefits of, 102
  impact on soda consumption,
    104
  opinions on, 107, *108*
  potential revenue from, 100

L
Lancet (journal), 35
Laufer-Cahana, Ayala, 51
Lavizzo-Mourey, Risa, 42
Le Pain Quotidien, 54
Leonhardt, David, 110
Levine, Susan, 39
Ludwig, David S., 44, 45, 99
Luik, John, 19
Lyons, Rob, 8, 46

M
Mass in Motion program, 58
Matthews, Jay, 70
McClellan, Mark, 83
McCullick, Bryan, 63
McDonald's, 54
McGinnis, J. Michael, 113
Mello, Michelle, 122
Metabolic syndrome, 27–28
Mitchell, Dan, 8
Moran, Jack, 54

N
National Association for Sport
  and Physical Education, 66
National Health and Nutrition
  Examination Survey, 20

Picture Credits

AJPhoto/Hopital de Pediatrie et de Reeducation de Bullion/Photo Researchers, Inc., 114
AP Images, 26, 48, 61, 65, 78, 85, 103
BSIP/Photo Researchers, Inc., 11
Bubbles Photo Library, 21
Cengage/Gale, 15, 22, 29, 41, 55, 59, 67, 77, 101, 108, 112
Jonathan Ernst/Reuters/Landov, 119
Gusto/Photo Researchers, Inc., 43
© Imagebroker/Alamy, 95
© Megapress/Alamy, 16
Dai Sugano/MCT/Landov, 88
Justin Sullivan/Getty Images, 50, 53
Alex Wong/Getty Images, 72

Alamance Community College
Library
P.O. Box 8000
Graham, NC 27253